WITHDRAWN
HARVARD LIBRARY
WITHDRAWN

KIERKEGAARD
Bernard Bykhovskii

PHILOSOPHICAL CURRENTS

Vol 16

David H. DeGrood

Editor

Joseph Bien	S. Daniel Melita
Leslie Berman Burger	Benjamin B. Page
Edward D'Angelo	John Pappademos
Marvin Farber	Raymond R. Rector
Nicole Fuyet	Dale Riepe
Jairus Gilden	Shingo Shibata
Stuart L. Hackel	William G. Stratton
James Lawler	Philip M. Zeltner

Associates

The important views expressed by our writers are represented without necessarily implying concurrence of either editors or publisher.

B. R. Grüner B.V.—Amsterdam—1976

Kierkegaard

by
Bernard Bykhovskii

Translated
by
Henry F. Mins

B. R. Grüner B.V.—Amsterdam—1976

© ISBN 90 6032 070 0

FOREWORD

Professor Bernard Bykhovskii has been well known for many years as an outstanding Marxist scholar. His contributions to the literature show him to be not only schooled in the thought of Marx, Engels, and Lenin, but also an indefatigable exponent of its application to themes warranting renewed treatment and to new subject matters which have emerged in the twentieth century. As his bibliography indicates, he has devoted much time to the history of philosophy, and to trends of thought which have become prominent in recent years, including phenomenology and existentialism. An uncompromising thinker and critic, he has vigorously defended a well-defined position, in contrast to the various forms of Marxist revisionism – overt and covert – which are now a widespread mode of manifestation of more deep-seated socioeconomic issues.

In the present book Professor Bykhovskii addresses himself to the thought of Kierkegaard, the Danish writer who posthumously has become a force in twentieth century religious and existential philosophy. Kierkegaard is viewed in connection with the line of development of idealism, beginning with his relationship to Schelling and Hegel. The severe account of the later Schelling is entirely fair. Owing his greatest claim to membership in the "great tradition" to his status early in his life as a predecessor of Hegel, by whom he was soon overshadowed, the later Schelling has received renewed attention as one of the forerunners of existential thought. How weak and unsuccessful the efforts of his last period were has been apparent to those who were able to appraise his final efforts with logical criteria.

Throughout the book passages from Kierkegaard's writings are quoted painstakingly and in pertinent detail, so that the reader is able to turn to the sources for further study. But the quotations are in themselves sufficiently detailed to justify the critical interpretation set forth. Where it appears called for, the positive historical significance of Kierkegaard is pointed out. That negative criticism predominates is to be expected from the evidence, which could easily have been added to in a more extended discussion.

It may be recalled that idealism continued to be a force following the rise of the sciences and the evolutionary literature of the nineteenth century, which were targets of its criticism; and that, because of its increasing influence, Marxist thought was treated as another object of criticism by writers in the established intellectual world. Thus the natural sciences were stereotyped and circumscribed by their critics, and the so-called cultural sciences, or the humanistic disciplines, were held to offer a haven of refuge for faith and philosophical autonomy, unrestricted by the findings of the sciences. Marxist thought generally met with unrelenting opposition, characteristically buttressed by modes of falsification compatible with dominant or special interests of the country in which the writer happened to be active.

Kierkegaard's text clearly shows his hostility to science; and his antiscientific spirit was to be seen in its full significance in more recent years. The intensity of his reaction to science is comparable to his attitude regarding existence. This is effectively portrayed by Professor Bykhovskii, who examines the most important elements of Kierkegaard's thought in order to make clear his sociohistorical motivation. In this task he appears as a careful critic, with only unavoidably brief indications of the nature of the principles he emphasizes, and has discussed elsewhere. In keeping with Kierkegaard's thought, which was greatly restricted by his own scholarly limitations and social preferences, the discussion highlights the nature of his subjectivism and his ethical-religious views. Not only is the argument supported at all times by passages from the primary sources, but also by the author's discerning attention to the abundant literature dealing with Kierkegaard, including American as well as European writers.

In accordance with his chosen historical perspective, the author observes that the "ethical stages" of Kierkegaard, which have intrigued so many readers of the religious and philosophical literature, had nothing in common with the development of ethics in the course of social existence; and he points out that Kierkegaard's conception of the ethical was merely embodied in subjective-personal diversity, and not in historical-evolutionary concreteness. The fact that the conception of man and the world employed by Kierkegaard violated basic truths about human and natural existence did not prevent it from being entertained, in schools of theology and elsewhere, as a desirable alternative to a science-oriented view. Thus man was said to be cast as into a pit, and into an alien and dismal world, with all being frightening him. This type of language has been all too familiar in the recent literature. The social consequences of the view that good health is a greater danger than wealth and power, or the doctrine that suffering and renunciation of the world are a blessing, can only be congenial to those who would leave the status quo unchallenged. Professor Bykhovskii is right in declaring the avowed apolitical character of

Kierkegaard's thought to be antipolitical, and in pointing out the actual consequences of his mode of detachment and subjective philosophy. On the basis of the evidence his thought is judged to be individualistic and antisocial. Kierkegaard's preference of the monarchical form of government shows him to be an acquiescent son of his social system. A subjective-religious philosophy can be readily seen to signify a means of flight from the actual world, in which vested inequalities and a class structure are allowed to stand. The very use of vacuous generalities may represent such a flight by avoiding all thought of social change, in effect if not explicitly. Professor Bykhovskii sees the doctrine of the primacy of the personality and the denial of politics as a form of political conservatism; and the Kierkegaardian turning to subjectivism may also be viewed as going along with the later subjectivistic requirements of nonparticipating observers and ideal impartiality, as "helping to retain the existing order of things."

The impact of this book is sure to be widely felt in the academic world and more generally by serious readers of the philosophical literature. It deserves the attention of such readers as an important critical addition to the available literature, which has so largely failed to see Kierkegaard in his actual historical relations and in the real significance of his thought. I take great pleasure in commending this excellent book and its eminent author to all who seek further enlightenment on the philosophical and ideological issues of our time.*

Special acknowledgment should be made to Dr. Henry F. Mins, the translator, and to Professor David DeGrood, the Series Editor, for their help in making this publication possible.

Marvin Farber

---

* Attention may be called to two articles by Professor Bykhovskii recently published in the international quarterly, *Philosophy and Phenomenological Research* (State University of New York at Buffalo), on "Marcusism against Marxism" in Dec. 1969, and "A Philosophy of Despair" in Dec. 1973.

TABLE OF CONTENTS

Foreword, Marvin Farber .... p. v
Chapter   I. The End of German Classical Philosophy ...... p. 1
Chapter   II. The Copenhagen Anomaly .... p. 16
Chapter III. Anti-Hegel .... p. 25
Chapter   IV. Pathetic Egocentrism .... p. 45
Chapter   V. The Crucifixion of Reason .... p. 51
Chapter   VI. Narcotic Ethics .... p. 69
Chapter VII. A Spy in the Service of the Lord .... p. 90
Chapter VIII. The Second Coming .... p. 109
Bibliography .... p. 117
About the Author .... p. 120

"There is only one single man who possesses the prerequisites permitting an authentic critique of my work: that is I myself."
"What I am standing on, my head or my feet, I do not know."
                                                                S. Kierkegaard

CHAPTER I

THE END OF GERMAN CLASSICAL PHILOSOPHY

Thursday, November 15, 1841. There was unusual animation that day on the Unter den Linden in Berlin near the Opernplatz. Coaches, carriages and pedestrians were all milling around. They were not going to the opera house but to the university, to Lecture Hall No. 6, the largest one in the university, which could not hold all those who wanted to attend, far more than its four hundred seats.

"If you ask anyone in Berlin today ...," Friedrich Engels, who was there at the time, wrote, "where the arena is on which the battle is being waged for domination of the public opinion of Germany in politics and religion ... he will answer that that arena is in the university, to be specific in Lecture Hall No. 6, where Schelling is giving his lectures on the philosophy of revelation." (1, 386) "Schelling's introductory lecture," the newspapers of the time wrote, "was read with the same curiosity in Germany as the speech from the throne." (81, 782)

There was just as large a crowd at the second lecture, which was attended by Sören Kierkegaard from Denmark. "Schelling began," he wrote to P. I. Spang on November 18, "but with so much noise and commotion, whistling, knocking on the windows by those who could not get into the crowed lecture hall...." "As to externals," Kierkegaard adds, "Schelling looks like the most ordinary man, like any cavalry captain...." (6, 35, 71)

But on subsequent days the audience shrank considerably. Interest in the lectures decreased: "...Schelling left almost all his hearers dissatisfied." (1, 395) He failed to live up to expectations. He did not score the expected triumph. "The great sensation proved to be only a sensation and, as such, left no trace." (60, 286) The mountain had given birth to a mouse.

On August 1, 1840, Friedrich-Wilhelm IV had ascended the throne. The echoes of the July Revolution of 1830 had not yet died away. The storms of 1848 were not far off.

It was soon ten years from the date of Hegel's death. His chair had been taken over by Gabler, a Right Hegelian epigone. But it was not he that inspired young minds, but Hegel, as before. "When Hegel died, his philosophy only began to live." (1, 396) "The period from 1830 to

1840 was the time of the unquestioned reign of 'Hegelianism,' " (2, 21, 279). The Left Hegelians, the "Hegelings," were the governors of the minds of the advanced German youth of those years. Remaining true to Hegel's basic principles, the Young Hegelians rejected the conclusions of the Hegelian system, which were not justified on those very principles. Their center at the University of Berlin was the group of the "Free:" Strauss, Bauer, the young Feuerbach, the still younger Engels. In its new form the philosophy of the official Prussian philosopher became the spiritual weapon of the mutinous spirits.

In Friedrich Wilhelm IV's eyes, strengthening the existing order had as its urgent ideological prerequisite the eradication of the "dragon's growth of Hegelian pantheism, deceptive pretensions to omniscience and lawless annihilation of domestic good order so as to achieve a scientifically based rebirth of the nation," as he wrote to von Bunsen (cited from 83, 782). War was declared on the "band of Hegelings" from above. By royal order the 66-year old Schelling was invited from Munich to play the part of St. George "and rout the fearful dragon of Hegelianism." (1, 395) In 1841, the year in which Strauss's *History of Christian Doctrines*, Bruno Bauer's *Critique of the Synoptics*, and Feuerbach's *Essence of Christianity* were published and Karl Marx defended his thesis on Democritus and Epicurus, Schelling moved to Berlin and began his lectures at Berlin University. He was given the title of senior governmental privy councilor and a salary of 4000 thalers. His courses of lectures on the philosophy of mythology and the philosophy of revelation continued until 1846, when Schelling reached the age of seventy-one. After 1841 Lecture Hall No. 6 was no longer required for his lectures. The number of auditors dropped catastrophically. He did not succeed in his mission as St. George. He died seven years later at the Swiss health resort of Ragatz.

It probably never entered the head of the Austrian ambassador in Berlin, Prince Metternich, that along with him in Lecture Hall No. 6, listening to Schelling's words of wisdom, was a furious rebel, a refugee from the Russian monarchy, who was to fight on the barricades of Vienna a few years later.

Mikhail Ivanovich Bakunin was impatient for Schelling's lectures to begin. "You can not imagine," he wrote home on November 3, 1841, "with what impatience I look forward to Schelling's lectures. For a year I have been reading a great deal of him and found in him such unfathomable depth of life, of creative thinking, that I am sure that now too he will disclose to us much that is deep. Thursday, that is tomorrow, he begins." (14, 3, 67)

But even the first long-awaited lecture, of which he had expected so much, clearly disappointed the twenty-seven year old revolutionary. "I am writing you in the evening, after Schelling's lecture," he writes his sister while still under the immediate impression (November 15, 1841), "Very interesting, but insignificant enough, with nothing that speaks to the heart, but I don't want to draw any conclusions yet; I want to hear him further without prejudgments." (14, 3, 78)

A year later, when the reactionary trend and theoretical poverty of the "philosophy of revelation" had been fully unfolded, Bakunin drew very definite conclusions, characterizing Schelling, in a letter to his brother on November 7, 1842, as "a miserable, living-dead romantic...." (14, 3, 439) The turbulent rebel, possessed by his revolutionary quests, was revolted by the theosophical exhortations of the aged philosopher betraying his past from his professorial chair.

On November 22, 1841 Kierkegaard wrote in his diary: "I am so glad, indescribably glad, that I heard Schelling's second lecture.... There is where clarification may come from.... Now I have placed all my hopes in Schelling...." (7, 148)

Alas, his hopes too were not realized. They faded away with every lecture. Patiently listening to thirty-six lectures, Kierkegaard did not finish the course. On February 27, 1842, he wrote his brother that "Schelling jabbers intolerable twaddle.... I think that I'll go completely silly if I keep on listening to Schelling."

More patient than Bakunin, Kierkegaard from his quite different position was just as decisively disillusioned with the Berlin Prophet. "In Berlin," we read in his diary, "it turns out, I have nothing more to do.... I am too old to listen to lectures and Schelling is too old to give them. His entire doctrine of potencies manifests complete impotence." (7, 154)

Having got nothing for his pains, Kierkegaard left Berlin and returned home. His trip had proved altogether fruitless.

It would be quite unjust to belittle and even more so to deny the positive significance of Schelling's early work in the evolution of classical German philosophy, and hence in the entire process of the history of philosophical thought. The doctrines of both Fichte and Schelling were steps rising from the foothills to the new historical form of dialectics, from the negative dialectics of the Kantian antinomies to the Hegelian summit of idealist dialectics. The transition from the subjectivistically and voluntaristically colored dialectics of Fichte to the dialectics of absolute idealism was mediated by the objective dialectics of Schelling in his *Naturphilosophie* and philosophy of identity. "But the fire went out, courage vanished, the fermenting must, failing to become pure wine, turn into vinegar." (1, 442) From being an active force in the development of philosophical thought, Schelling turned into a force opposing that development.

This took place long before the lectures in Berlin. Friedrich Wilhelm IV had good reasons for putting his money, in the fight against progressive ideas, on the philosopher from Munich, "whose memory blooms unfading in the annals of German thought...." (18, 6, 134), for all of Schelling's subsequent activity was directed towards eradicating what his hands had sown.

With his usual wit, penetration and pitilessness, Heinrich Heine talked to his French readers of the Schelling of the Munich period: "There I saw him wandering around like a ghost, I saw his big colorless eyes and doleful face, devoid of expression – a sad spectacle of fallen splendor." (18, 6, 134)

Heine, however, saw only the subjective motives for Schelling's hostility to the philosophical doctrine of his former friend, who had raised dialectical thought to heights never reached before. "Just as a shoemaker will talk about another shoemaker and accuse him of stealing leather from him and making it up into boots, so I chanced to meet Mr. Schelling and heard how he talked about Hegel – Hegel, who had 'taken his ideas.' 'It was my ideas he took,' and once again, 'my ideas' – that was the continual drone of this poor man. To tell the truth, if the shoemaker Jakob Böhme spoke like a philosopher in the old days, Schelling the philosopher talks today like a shoemaker." (18, 6, 212)

Like all the advanced thinkers of that time, Heine could not forgive Schelling for "betraying philosophy for the sake of the Catholic religion," (18, 6, 213) replacing logical clarity of thought by the mist of "mystical intuition," of the immediate contemplation of the absolute. But Heine did not take into consideration the objective side of the matter: after what Hegel had accomplished, no further development of dialectical thought was possible either along the lines of the idealism that was a constant of classical German philosophy, nor on the basis of the bourgeois Weltanschauung out of which that philosophy grew. The only way to go beyond Hegel's philosophy was to leave that basis and abandon the idealist camp built on it. That was something Schelling was incapable of doing; he preferred to leave the path of rational, logical knowledge. "This is where philosophy ends with Mr. Schelling and poetry, I should say foolishness, begins...." (18, 6, 131) This was said in 1834. Schelling's path from Munich to Berlin was laid out long before 1841.

Schelling's departure from the path of classical German philosophy was criticized at the outset by Hegel himself, in the *Science of Logic*, in which he condemned the betrayal of science and logic by those "who, as if firing a pistol, start off directly from their internal revelation, from faith, intellectual contemplation, and so forth, and want to divorce themselves from method and logic." (17, 1, 124) These words seize the very essence of the turnabout made by Schelling, from rationalism to irrationalism, from philosophy to theosophy.

The great service rendered by German classic philosophy, which reached its utmost development in Hegel's dialectical idealism, was the foundation of a new and higher historical form of rationalism, eliminating the metaphysical and formal-logical limitations of previous rationalism. Dialectical logic conquered the dynamic and contradictory forms of being which were previously regarded as inaccessible to rational knowledge and logical thought, and inadmissible by them. It infinitely expanded the sphere in which logic has jurisdiction, opening up a boundless perspective for rationalism.

For Hegel, "faith in the power of reason is the first condition of philosophical studies.... The secret essence of the Universe has no force within it that could offer resistance to the boldness of knowledge...." (16, 1, 16) Hegel repeats, over and over again, this deepest conviction of his, the Ariadne's thread of his entire philosophy. The dialectical rearming of logic was what assured this power of thought. The Hegelian dialectic, which was later so mutilated by the neo-Hegelians, falsely presented by them as going beyond the boundaries of the rational, was in fact a new historical flight of rationalism. As early as in the *Phenomenology of Spirit* Hegel proclaimed that what is not rational lacks all reality.

"Hegel's faith in human reason and its rights" (3, 2, 7) was inseparably linked, not with any going beyond the boundaries of rationalism, but with the elimination of metaphysical limits to the course of rational knowledge. That is why for Hegel the idealist, as for his heirs, Schelling's lurch into irrationalism was "bad idealism."

But the sterile flower of the philosophy of revelation that had grown in Munich blossomed out fully only in Berlin after being transplanted into the hothouse of the Prussian monarchy. There too it encountered the furious opposition of all those who had gone through the school of Hegel, both the Right and the Left Hegelians. Two months after Schelling's lectures had begun, Kierkegaard wrote to Pastor Spang (January 8, 1842): "The Hegelians are fanning the flame. Schelling looks as gloomy as if he had been pickled in vinegar." (6, 35, 86) The reference is to the attacks of the Right Hegelian Michelet on Schelling in the introduction to the second volume of Hegel's "Encyclopedia of Philosophical Sciences." But in the avant-garde of the counterattack on the philosophy of revelation there marched an as yet unknown Young Hegelian named Friedrich Engels. This was the first Left Hegelian utterance against neo-Schellingianism.

In the fall of 1841, just in time for Schelling's lectures, Engels was in Berlin to do his military service. "Incidentally," he wrote Arnold Ruge in reply to an invitation to make a critique of Schelling's utterances, "I am not a doctor of any kind and cannot become one; I am only a businessman and a Royal Prussian artilleryman." (1, 513) But Engels's negative attitude towards Schelling had been formulated even before his transfer to Berlin. As early as 1840, in his article on *Immerman's Memoirs*, Engels poses a rhetorical question hitting at the essence of Schelling's turning away from classical philosophy: "Is not all philosophy cut short where the correspondence of thinking and the empirical 'goes beyond the concept'? What logic can stand up...?" (1, 382)

Schelling's break with Hegel, his anti-Hegelianism, was the turning point in the history of German philosophical idealism and a presage of a similar turn in all bourgeois philosophy in general. Engels, hearing Schelling's lectures, could not yet see the maturing crisis of philosophical idealism but he made a very determined attack on the abandoment planned by Schelling of the rational form of thought. At this point there was a chasm between the idealisms of Hegel and Schelling. "Two old friends in their youth, roommates at the Tübingen theological seminary, meet again face to face as adversaries forty years later. One died ten years ago but is alive today, more than any one else, in his writings; the other... has been spiritually dead for three decades by now, when he suddenly professes to have full vitality, and demands recognition." (1, 386) The core of the dispute was that Hegel was proud of reason (cf. 1, 451), while Schelling limited and disparaged it.

Engels was not by any means an adherent of orthodox Hegelianism. He noted that Hegel was under attack from two opposite sides, "from the side of his predecessor Schelling and from the side of his younger successor Feuerbach." (1, 443) In referring to Feuerbach, Engels makes no secret of his sympathy for atheistic anthropologism and his intolerance of "Schelling's scholastic-mystical mode of thought." (1, 413) However, Engels's critical attitude towards Hegel from the left, opposing the critique of Hegel from the right, had not yet ripened into a critique of philosophical idealism from the position of the opposite camp in philosophy; he had not yet broken with the Young Hegelians. His criticism of Schelling brings him close to Left Hegelianism rather than divorcing him from it.* But a further, and decisive, swing can already be seen in his orientation towards Feuerbach.

A year after Ruge had approached Engels, Karl Marx made the same proposal to Feuerbach, seeing in him the true antipodes of Schelling.

---

* In his *Philosophical-historical Lexicon* L. Noack attributes Engels's *Schelling, the Philosopher in Christ* to Bruno Bauer. (83, 783)

Marx's attitude towards neo-Schellingianism was clear and unequivocal. "Schelling's philosophy is Prussian policy *sub specie philosophiae*." (2, 27, 377) He had no doubt that Feuerbach would be ready to denounce the retrograde doctrine that Feuerbach in his *Essence of Christianity* had called "the philosophy of the guilty conscience," whose innermost secret was "groundless, childish fantasy." Its motto was: "the more absurd, the deeper." (24, 2; 28, 223) "Poor Germany," Feuerbach exclaimed in the preface to his anti-religious masterpiece, "you have often been misled in the field of philosophy, and you have been deceived most often by the above mentioned Cagliostro, who has constantly fooled you..." (24, 2, 29). And although Feuerbach, who was engaged in other work at the time, declined Marx's request, his letters in reply give a clear picture of his contempt for Schelling's university preachings, and his militant antagonism to theosophical elucubrations.

Schelling did not publish his five years of Berlin courses of lectures, and his manuscripts, which had remained all but unstudied, were lost during World War II in the ruins of the Munich university library in the course of the bombings in Summer 1944. The basic source of our knowledge of the contents of the Berlin lectures are the notes taken by auditors. One such was Kierkegaard's synopsis, discovered by Eva Nordentoft-Schlecht in the Danish National Library and published for the first time (in a German translation) in 1962. (71) But since Kierkegaard attended only the mythological portion of Schelling's course (forty-one lectures), its crowning section, the *Philosophy of Revelation*, is not found in that synopsis. Nonetheless, we are extremely interested in six lectures (9–15) in which, criticizing Hegel's philosophy, Schelling committed the suicide of German classical idealism in the person of one of its founders.

A profound conviction of the rationality of reality was the guiding principle of Hegel's entire philosophical structure. And it was precisely that principle that was the basic target of Schelling's anti-Hegelian attacks. But the principle involves two interpretations: the panlogical confidence in the rational nature of the movement and development of everything that exists, a confidence that calls for its rational understanding, and an apologetic interpretation of being as it is, with the resultant conservative outcomes of the Hegelian system. The first interpretation of the principle of rationality of all reality is treated by Hegel as idealistic identity of being and concept, of the real and the logical. The "logic of things" is understood not metaphorically, as objective regularity, requiring logical understanding and accessible only to such understanding, but in the literal sense, as ontological identity of being and development as the logic of the world reason, the absolute idea.

The objective of Schelling's attack on the principle of the rationality of the real was not idealistic identity nor its apologetic undercurrent, but the rationalist, logical dominant. The focus of his anti-Hegelian critique was philosophical rationalism, which in Hegel took the radical form of panlogism. Severance of the real and the rational, contraposition of the logical to the real, denial that being is methodologically accessible to rational knowledge: these are the basic premises of Schelling's "philosophy of revelation," which he sets up against Hegel.

Schelling rejects Hegelianism *in toto*. In his opinion, Hegel was only an unfortunate episode in the history of modern philosophy. In trying to transform logic into a science that opened the way to the absolute, in identifying the logical with the actual, Hegel, in Schelling's words, made a fool of himself (*sich zum Narren machte*, Lecture 10). His panlogism exalts philosophy above religion, since "purely rational knowledge can no more be Christian than geometry can." (Lecture 13) Christianity is so rarefied in his theory that it is hardly recognizable. (Lecture 18) What kind of theism is this, anyway, if the absolute idea loses all personal character? (Lecture 15) How can such a philosophy pretend to be Christian? It is to be rejected as the worthless product of a false method "which collapses disgracefully in the passage to real being." (25, 7, 891)

The root of the evil, Schelling asserts, lies in the fact that logic meddles in what does not concern it, going beyond the boundaries of what is accessible to it. It can reach only the *possible*, not the *actual*. When it pretends to knowledge of the latter, it inevitably fails, manifesting its impotence. Excluding the actual, the existent, real being from the sphere of logical knowledge, Schelling opposes to it a different, non-logical kind of knowledge, extending not to possibility but to actuality. The actual, according to Schelling, becomes the object of philosophy when philosophy is guided neither by what is given in thought nor what is given in sense experience. "Its principle cannot be either experience nor pure thought." (Lecture 17) He has a higher experience in view – "intellectual intuition," pretersensual contemplation. Engels' statements in his article *Immerman's Memoirs*, mentioned above, note this irrationalist, essentially mystical trend in Schelling's postulate, according to which the concordance of thought and the empirical "goes beyond the limits of the concept."

"Schelling," Kierkegaard wrote to Bösen on December 14, 1861, "defends his discovery to the effect that there are two philosophies: a negative and a positive." But "Hegel does not belong in either one – it is just refined Spinozism." (6, 35, 75) By the negative philosophy, which in contrast to Hegelianism has some right to existence within certain limits, Schelling means his previous philosophy of identity. But in and of itself the negative philosophy is not yet the true, full-valued philosophy, only the prelude to it. The negative philosophy is fettered to reason, the positive philosophy discloses philosophy. And the greatest error of Hegel is that he takes an uncritical attitude towards the negative philosophy, in Schelling's opinion, absolutizes it, thereby transforming it into what it should not and cannot be, presenting the possible as the actual and the actual as the rational, logical.

Really, according to Schelling, the negative philosopy, correctly understood and properly evaluated, requires its own surmounting. In this consists the adequate self-knowledge of the negative philosophy. "The negative philosophy ends by requiring the positive...." "The negative philosophy attains its triumph in the positive philosophy." (Lectures 14 and 20) The former, as self-limitation of a reason that has reached its limit, serves as a bridge to the second.

What is the relationship of the positive philosophy to reason? The answer to this question, which is decisive for Schelling, is the line of demarcation between the two philosophies. In the negative philosophy, he says, reason is correlated only with itself, whereas in the positive philosophy it enters into relation with reality itself. Thus the irrationality of being is counterposed to the rationality of logical thought.

What we have here is a critique, from the right, of the historical accomplishment of dialectical idealism, which set up a logic capable of knowing the rationality of what many previously (and Schelling subsequently) regarded as irrational in being itself. Hegel's idealistic deformation of being, his identification of it with thought, are here criticized not for idealism but for rationalism. Logic is rejected not because it pretends to primacy with respect to actuality but because it pretends to attain actuality, to express it adequately.

Engels already called attention to the fact that when Schelling accuses reason of "not being able to know anything actual," he has in mind primarily the inaccessibility to reason of "God and the secret of Christianity." (1, 449) For Schelling the fundamental defect of rational knowledge is that it "has nothing to say about religion, real religion, which it does not contain even as a possibility." (Lecture 14) Schelling conducts his critique of dialectical logic from the position of metaphysical irrationalism. Philosophy degenerates into theosophy.

Logical necessity is nothing other than natural-historical regularity abstracted from the nature of things and reworked in the human brain. Determinism is an inseparable integral element of dialectical logic, despite the different ways in which it is understood in idealist and in materialist dialectics. But determinism in dialectical logic, with its principle of self-movement, is qualitatively diverse from metaphysical and mechanistic determinism, which gravitates towards fatalism.

Schelling, rejecting the rationality of being along with panlogism, discards both logical necessity and universal regularity, resuscitating the metaphysical antimony of freedom and necessity. While the negative philosophy, as the doctrine of essence, is a system of necessity and rationalism, the positive philosophy in contrast, as the doctrine of existence, is a system of freedom and revelation (cf. 71 and 74). In his 24th lecture Schelling asserted that this view of the question does not in any way stand in contradiction to dialectics; on the contrary, "strictly speaking, dialectics belongs to freedom and hence to positive philosophy." But in this interpretation dialectics loses its character as dialectical logic and ceases to be what it is in fact, the highest form of rationalism. Dialectics degenerates into its contrary (as it does later in neo-Hegelian irrationalism), into alogism. Alogism in Schelling assumes the unmistakable form of mysticism, miraculous divine arbitrariness ruling over actuality.

What becomes of the Christian categories in the purely logical world of necessity? Schelling asks pointblank. (cf. 71, 22) Freedom stands up against necessity, as a Christian category against a logical category. As against self-motion as the immanent logic of being, we have creation, "based on the will of God." "Will is the primal being *(Ursein).*" (Lecture 27)

Thus Schelling, breaking with dialectical logic and rationalism in general, represents actuality not as a sphere of objective regularity accessible to reason, but as the arena of divine providence.

The prodigal son of classical German philosophy throws away all its achievements, while wrapping his philosophy of revelation in an ephemeral envelope which in his hands becomes an empty and dead triadic pattern. In Hegel the dialectical triad, for all its forced schematism, had within it the principle of double negation as the general law of progressive development; in Schelling it takes on a decorative-mythological character. Where Hegel sought to resolve the mythological forms of Christian dogma into logical concepts, Schelling performs the reverse motion from logical categories to mythological phantasmagorias.

His triadic schemes are a world removed from the triadic constructions of Hegel, in which there pulses the contradictory unity of the negative and the positive. The two men are as far from each other as dialectical negation from the divine trinity.

The doctrine of the three potencies is a parody by Schelling on the dialectical triad. He formulates a religious triad: mythology, the Christian mysteries, the philosophy of revelation, as the three stages of religious consciousness. The history of the Christian Church too takes on triadic form in Schelling: Catholicism, the church of the Apostle Peter; Protestantism, the church of the Apostle Paul; and the church of universal love, the church of the Apostle John. Engels gives us the closing words of Schelling's course, which Kierkegaard was no longer there to hear: "...at some time a church will be built to all three apostles, and that church will be the last, truly Christian Pantheon." (1, 459) But in his 36th lecture Schelling reaches the *nec plus ultra* by way of a parody, forming a triad of original sin, in which the thesis is the temptation of man, the antithesis the complaisance of woman, and the synthesis the serpent as the principle of temptation. Only a step from the sublime to the ridiculous. This is what became of dialectics in the philosophy of revelation (a philosophy which, Schelling held, was worthy of being called the "Christian philosophy"), which set as its goal not the *proof* of the truth of the Christian religion, which does not need proof (Lecture 32), but the elucidation, the disclosure of divine revelation taken on faith.

The entries in Kierkegaard's diary, and his letters, leave no doubt that Schelling' lectures were a bitter disappointment to him, but by themselves they do not explain why this was so, why the disillusionment was so strong that it drove him to leave Berlin and return to Copenhagen without finishing the course. It would seem that Schelling's relentless critique of Hegelian logicism, and his "Christian philosophy", should have attracted such an ardent proponent of Christianity as Kierkegaard. Did not the irrationalist course that Kierkegaard took accord with the basic trend to depart from classical German idealism that characterized the philosophy of revelation? Did not the exorcising of the "negative philosophy" appeal to Kierkegaard?

Clearly, the irrationalistic hostility to Hegelianism was a point of contact of the two philosophers. But there were both quantitative and essential qualitative differences in their breaks with the classical tradition of German idealism.

In the first place, Schelling's rupture with his own philosophical past was neither consistent nor unconditional. "Negative philosophy" was limited but not thrown overboard from philosophy; it kept a subordinate, auxiliary role. "Positive philosophy" bridled and condemned rationalism but did not yet break with it definitively. Schelling counterposed the "positive" and "negative" philosophies but was unwilling to liquidate the latter irrevocably (cf. 32, 238). Engels observed that "Schelling, with all the services he renders to true Christianity, still cannot completely surrender his previous false wisdom.... He still cannot totally give up his pride in his own reason...." (1, 448)

Kierkegaard was repelled by the "survivals" of rationalism and logicism in Schelling, his residual tendency towards "systematization," for which Kierkegaard later reproached both Hegel and Schelling. But this criticism of system-making was not conducted from the left, from the point of view of consistent application of dialectical logic, but from the right, in the name of eliminating the very logical nature of the philosophical construct. For the Copenhagen preacher of "true Christianity," the mere idea of "theosophical theo*logy*" was intolerable. Schelling, rising to the heights of religion, has not discarded all the burdensome "ballast" of logisms and sophisms. He was not radical enough in his irrationalism. The "philosophy of revelation" was complemented in him by "Christo*logy*" and "Satano*logy*." "...As the result of pretentious speculative interpretation, all of Christian terminology," in Kierkegaard's words, "is distorted beyond recognition." Kierkegaard calls this a "prostitution of all mythology." (6, 11–12, 79)

Not only did Kierkegaard maintain a more consistent irrationalism, but in contrast to Schelling he directed his irrationalism on the subjective-idealist path rather than on the objective-idealist one, thereby expressing a more decisive departure from the culminating phase of German classical idealism. "Schelling brought self-reflection to a halt, regarding intellectual intuition not as a discovery within reflection, and as attainable in the course of constant advance, but as a new point of departure." (6, 16, II, 38) Schelling's revelation is extroverted, directed outwards; it claims that it expresses the divine potencies, that it is *knowledge of God*. Kierkegaard's philosophy, to the contrary, excludes any such possibility. The objectivistic theocentrism of the "philosophy of revelation" was alien and intolerable to Kierkegaard. His religious faith was based on subjectivistic egocentrism. To the Schellingian divine potencies as passions of the Lord he opposes human passions, leading to the mysterious beyond.

Kierkegaard had already left Berlin when Schelling lamented that scholars "who know by heart all the species of infusoria and every chapter of Roman law...as a result forget about eternal salvation, in which the felicity of souls lies." (1, 460) This tirade of Schelling's, harmonizing with Kierkegaard's cast of mind, was not the focal point of the "philosophy of revelation" and is peripheral to Schelling's system as a whole. The antithesis contained in it became the axis of a different Christian philosophy – Kierkegaard's existentialism.

Schelling's lectures did not touch Kierkegaard "to the quick;" they left him cold, indifferent, a strange to the labored theosophical constructs. They did convince him that what is needed to overcome the philosophy of the Enlightenment, scientific knowledge and logical thought is not Schellingian revelation but another spritual weapon made of an altogether, irrationalistic material. Kierkegaard's critique of neo-Schellingianism, in contradistinction to Schelling's critique of Hegel, is not a critique of its theosophical form from the standpoint of rationalistic objective idealism, but a critique of objective idealism from the position of a complete *subjectivistic* fideism.

November 15, 1841 is a significant date in the history of German philosophy, the day, as it were, of the official internment of the progressive trend in philosophical idealism after it had reached the limits of its creative possibilities. That day marked the beginning of the downward path of rationalist thought in idealist philosophy on the inclined plane of irrationalism – from Hegel to the three "Sch"s: Schelling, Schleiermacher, Schopenhauer.*

The "philosophy of revelation" proclaimed from the professorial chair at Berlin University did not, however, become the general line of irrationalism. In anathematizing the legacy of classical German philosophy Schelling marked the end of the progressive development of idealist philosophy, but he did not become the guide of future generations of idealists into the misty future, on *Holzwege*,** to nowhere. "The philosophy of revelation, once so eagerly awaited, finally appeared, and when it did, bypassed its epoch without leaving a trace, as its epoch did it." (25, 768)

Through neo-Hegelianism, which distorted Hegel's dialectics and transformed it into its own irrationalist contrary; through the "tragical dialectics," with its principle of the irrationality of reality; through the stillborn "philosophy of life," irrationalism ran out into the channel of existentialism, whose idol was the disillusioned auditor of Schelling, a man who had been laughed at or forgotten for half a century. Criticism of the "philosophy of revelation" from the right, dissatisfaction with the degree and character of its irrationalism, became the starting point of the anti-scientific bourgeois philosophy, the *anti-philosophy* of our century. Denmark, a philosophical province of Germany a hundred years ago, became the Bethlehem of one of the dominant trends in contemporary idealism. Kierkegaardianism "proved its value" as the most effective spiritual narcotic in today's world.

But despite the great divergency between Kierkegaard's existentialism and the "philosophy of revelation," they have a vital spiritual affinity, a kinship in ideas. "In no other epoch has this genuine philosophy been as necessary as in the modern epoch of decadence." These words were written by none other than Karl Jaspers for the centennial of the death

---

* Kierkegaard refers to the "deathless services" of Schleiermacher, contraposing him to Hegel. (6, 11–12, 17) Schopenhauer, he writes, "is certainly a remarkable writer, who interested me greatly, and it surprised me, despite our complete divergence, to find a writer so close to me." (7, 2, 344)

** Impassable roads, wilds. Title of a book by M. Heidegger.

of Schelling and "the philosophy of revelation." (62, 31) The existentialist "philosophy of faith" and the all-embracing *(Umgreifende)* perspective bring out the kinship in ideas between Jaspers's Weltanschauung and that of the "positive philosophy." But the closest and most solid line of heritage appears in existentialism's highly negative attitude towards what Schelling called "negative philosophy" – in its departure from the way of rational, scientifically directed, objective knowledge.

Schelling died only a year earlier than Kierkegaard, but Kierkegaard outlived him by a full century. But in recent years voices have been heard, calling for a revision of the solidly-established traditional place assigned the late Schelling in the history of philosophy, his role in the evolution of classical German idealism. Whatever the attitude of the several historians of philosophy may have been to the doctrines of the individual representatives of this idealism, it has been recognized as beyond question that its high point was Hegel's doctrine, while "the philosophy of Schelling, although it grew out of German idealism, ...marks a breach with the idealistic system of reason." (71, 23) "It is a firmly established principle of classification in the history of philosophy that German idealism reached its highpoint in the system of Hegel." (92, 239) Taking note of this indubitable fact and making reference to R. Kroner, W. Schultz, a Heidelberg philosopher, calls for subjecting this generally accepted proposition to question and revision. "It is this opinion," he adds, "that we intend to call into question here with the aid of consideration of the philosophy of the late Schelling...." (92, 239) "Of course," he says further on, "in the process we shall have to revise the notions as to German idealism that we have become accustomed to." (92, 241)

At the end of this revision the "philosophy of revelation" is presented by Schultz not as the death-throes of philosophical idealism but as its lawful coronation. For the highest point in the progress of reason, Schultz asserts after Schelling, is its self-limitation, the establishment of the bounds of its validity. In proclaiming this, the prophet of the positive philosophy did not betray the philosophy of reason but reached its heights. Irrationalism is thus presented as the lawful historical successor of rationalism and its only worthy heir. From this point of view, the contribution of German classical philosophy to the history of the development of philosophical thought is that Kant, Fichte and Hegel, step by step, brought thought closer to realizing its own limitation. The strength of their reason lies in their gradual coming to awareness of its unreason.

The rational core of this irrational conception of the history of philosophy is the involuntary and indirect recognition of the limited possibilities for the progress of substantial philosophical thought *along the paths of idealism*.

Schelling would have been right in his criticism of Hegel if he had asserted not the unrealizability of the transition from logically sublimated possibility to the illusory "reality" of the pretersensual world, but rather the impossibility of reaching real actuality from the closed circle of absolute idealism. He would have been right if he had brought to light the groundlessness of regarding the material world as other-being of spiritual substance, as an *embodiment* of the logical Idea. But if Schelling had taken the field against Hegel from such a position, he would not have been Schelling but anti-Schelling. That is why the critique of Hegelianism from the left, from materialist positions, not only did not exclude but included and heightened intolerance for Schellingianism.

"With Hegel," says Jaspers, "something came to an end" (60, 309). But Hegel's idealist dialectics was at once an end and a beginning. It led to a crossroads from which two roads left in two diametrically opposite directions. German classical idealism had exhausted its possibilities. A revolutionary situation had arisen in the history of social thought, conditioned of course not only by the immanent development of philosophy but founded on the deep social changes of the middle of last century.

Schelling's Berlin lectures marked the end of classical German idealism. But this was only the beginning of the end of the movement of philosophical idealism onto a rationalist path. The anti-Schellingian utterances of Feuerbach, Engels and Marx heralded the beginning of a revolutionary turn in the history of philosophy. The great conquest of classical German philosophy, dialectical logic, was not discarded as useless but became the Ariadne's thread of further philosophical progress for the creators of the new historical form of materialism, for "the materialistic friends of Hegelian dialectics." (3, 45, 30)

CHAPTER II

THE COPENHAGEN ANOMALY

"...Not only my works, but my life as well, the fitful intimacy of its entire mechanism, will be the subject of innumerable investigations," Kierkegaard foresaw. (8, II, 173) It would be hard to name any other philosopher whose personal life and creative work were so indissolubly connected as Sören Kierkegaard. Hegel's *Science of Logic* or Kant's *Critique of Pure Reason* are not expressions of their authors' personal life and do not draw attention to their intimate experiences. Understanding of the feelings and way of life of their creators is in no way requisite for an understanding of their philosophical creations. "It is hard to tell the life history of Immanuel Kant," wrote Heinrich Heine. "For he had no life and no history." (18, 6, 96) But just as much has been written about Kierkegaard's personal life as about his opinions. His opinions themselves were so autobiographical that in studying them it is impossible not to take his experiences, feelings, emotions into account. They are deeply emotional and as a rule are of the nature of sublimations of his anxieties and uneasiness. "I am reflexion from one end to the other," he wrote. (6, 33, 79) "In everything I have written, the topic is solely and exclusively myself." (6, 16, II, 331) All his literary production is egocentric to the highest degree; it was not unfair for a caricature in the Copenhagen satirical journal *Korsar* to have the heading: "The entire Universe revolves around Sören Kierkegaard."

And yet, if we look at his life with the eyes of our contemporaries, how petty, wretched, paltry the cares and anxieties of the Danish thinker appear, how exaggerated and hypertrophied (by him and those who have investigated him) are the insignificant episodes of the despondent and uneventful life of the "hermit genius," as he described himself with his characteristic bitter irony. In the last analysis, all his troubles were the morbid burrowing within his own soul of a man who was wrought up, unbalanced, wrapped up in himself, infinitely alone, devoured by his loneliness. "What would be trifles for anybody else are events of enormous significance for me...." (7, 161)

In Copenhagen, enclosed with its 120,000 inhabitants in its fortified ramparts, Kierkegaard shut himself up as if in an ivory tower. Neither the reaction that weighed upon Europe in the years of the Holy Alliance nor the revolutionary waves of 1848, which rolled even as far as to Denmark, aroused Kierkegaard, did not get him "out of himself," did not distract him from contemplation of himself, from living in and for himself. "Like a solitary pine, egoistically secluded within itself and striving upward, there I stand, not even casting a shadow, and only a single wild pigeon makes his nest in my branches," he wrote in his *Diary*. (7, 82) Solitude was his element: he sought and found his felicity in "being alone, literally alone in the immense world." (6, 33, 70)

Sören Aabye Kierkegaard was born in Copenhagen on May 5, 1813 (on the same day on which, five years later, Karl Marx was born – a thinker of quite a different stamp and on a different level). His father was fifty-seven, his mother forty-five. He was the seventh and last child of the family. Sören's father, Mikael Pedersen, was a shepherd in Jutland in his early years. At twelve he was taken to Copenhagen, where he began work as a clerk in his uncle's haberdashery. As he grew up and mastered merchandising, he started a commercial career on his own and soon got rich in the hosiery business. Owning six shops in Copenhagen and a large fortune, Kierkegaard's father retired from business at forty and lived on the interest of his capital. The year in which his youngest son was born, a year of government bankruptcy and devaluation in Denmark, did not affect Mikael, whose money was placed in solid securities.

Kierkegaard's mother Anna had been a servant in his father's house. Mikael Kierkegaard married her soon after the death of his first wife, and a child was born to them sooner than the law provides.

Mikael Pedersen was a morose, gloomy, strict man, a religious fanatic who devoted himself, after retiring from business, to praying and repenting his sins. Two "major sins" weighed on him, clouding his entire existence. These sins were a secret to Sören for a long time but when he learned of them later, they had a crushing effect. The father's first sin was a curse he had once addressed to the Lord God who had condemned the ten-year old shepherd to unbearably heavy work. His second sin was the seduction of the servant who later became his wife. "I was born as the result of a crime, I appeared against the will of God...", his youngest son wrote in his *Diary*, shortly before his death. For Sören's father prayed up to his death at ninety-two for forgiveness of these great sins which threatened him with the tortures of hell; thereby he turned forty years of his life into a hell indeed.

All of young Sören's education was under the determinant and constant influence of his father. "From childhood," he wrote later, "I was in the power of an intolerable despotism.... When I was little, I was given a strict and rigorous Christian education, humanly speaking, a dreadful education...." (6, 33, 75) The morose tutor undoubtedly had an enormous influence on his pupil. "If you...want to know how I became the kind of writer I am, I reply that I owe it to that old man, a person to whom I owe more than anyone else...", says an 1849 entry in Kierkegaard's *Diary*. (7, 381)

At six Sören went to school. A puny, sickly child, with curvature of the spine and thin bandy legs, he did not lack for taunters and practical jokers, and gave back as good as he got. Sören's father called the combative and caustic boy "the fork." In the fall of 1830, in obedience to his father, the seventeen-year old Sören registered as a student in the theological faculty of Copenhagen University. Like every student, he was enrolled in the royal bodyguard but was discharged in three days because of the state of his health. Despite his father's wishes, theology did not interest the young student. "I vainly seek," he wrote in the *Diary* he began in 1834, "something that might animate me. Even the sonorous language of the Middle Ages is unable to fill the hollowness forming within me." (7, 84) Esthetics attracted him more, and his studies in the theological faculty dragged on for a full ten years. For a short time, while a student, he taught Latin at a *Gymnasium*, and only in 1840 passed his last university examination.

The life this long-term student led was altogether out of keeping with his education. He lived in the dissipated rakish way of young Bohemians, preferring drinking parties in restaurants with his friends and going to the opera to serious occupations and study of theological treatises; his father patiently paid all the debts of his "prodigal son."

But inevitably this life as an idler and rake led to dissatisfaction, disillusionment and depression, from which Sören was released by an unexpected acquaintance. This was a fourteen-year old girl, Regina Olsen, whom the twenty-four year old Kierkegaard met for the first time in May of 1837. They were beings whose natures differed totally. "There was an infinite difference between her and me," he wrote later. (8, II, 381) She was direct, cheerful, lively, and he was nervous, ironical, affected. But extremes meet. They fell in love. "For half a year I felt more poetry within myself than in all the novels put together." (7, 168) It was his first and last love. Three years after they met they became engaged. But the day after his betrothal, as his *Diary* attests, Sören already had doubts about it. Just a year later, unexpectedly and inexplicably for Regina, she got the engagement ring back with a letter of farewell. "Forgive a man who, if he is good for anything, is unable to make a girl happy." (6, 15, 350) Regina was in despair. Sören was inexorable. But for long years after breaking irrevocably with Regina the breach weighed heavily on him; to the end of his life his spirit was faithful to his only love: "...I love her,

I never loved anyone else and I will not." (6, 15, 339) "There are only two people who meant so much to me," he wrote eight years after the break, "my deceased father and our dear little Regina, who also in a certain sense is dead to me." (6, 35, 225) He tried to meet her on the street and in church. He wrote letters to her. He kept coming back to it in his diary and literary works. "Not a day has passed since then on which I did not think of her from morning to night," we read in the *Diary*, five years after the breaking of the engagement (8, II, 24) And three years on: "Yes, you were my love, my only love, I loved you most of all when I had to desert you." (8, III, 188) In the draft of an unsent letter to Regina, written in 1849, we read: "*I thank you for the time when you were mine. I thank you for everything that I owe to you....* I thank you for your naiveté, you my fascinating teacher, I thank you for everything I learned, if not from your wisdom, then from your charm...." (6, 35, 244)

Six years after the break Regina married her former teacher and admirer Fritz Schlegel, who later became the Danish governor of the Virgin Islands. "She has married.... When I read about this in the newspaper, it was as though I had had a stroke...." (6, 5–6, 88) Kierkegaard wrote a letter to Schlegel: "In this life she will belong to you. She will enter into history along with me." (6, 35, 231) He devoted two of his *Edifying Discourses* to her. He left her all his property. Regina Schlegel outlived Kierkegaard for half a century and died at 82. "He sacrificed me to God," she wrote not long before her death. (6, 35, 278)

What fantastic conjectures Kierkegaard specialists have made in trying to explain the break! Some have imputed it to Kierkegaard's impotence; others have compared it to Abraham's offering his only son up in sacrifice.

Kierkegaard's writings contain some ideas on marriage that shed light on his bizarre conduct. "Many men have become geniuses thanks to a girl, many men have become heroes thanks to a girl, many men have become poets thanks to a girl, many men have become saints thanks to a girl, but who actually became a genius, a hero, a poet or a saint thanks to the girl who became his wife? ...Thanks to her he only became a councilor of commerce..a general...father of a family." (6, 15, 61) "Marrying, having children, getting hemorrhoids, passing the examination in theology, being elected a deputy...." (4, 232), and here is a frank admission: if I had married Regina, "I could never have become myself." (8, II, 381)

Such was the most important event in the private life of Kierkegaard, to whose biography innumerable dissertations have been devoted!

The break with Regina took place two weeks after Kierkegaard had defended his master's thesis "On the Concept of Irony, with Especial Attention to Socrates." Later, Kierkegaard called himself "Master of Irony." The dissertation displays not only careful study of Plato's Socratic dialogues but knowledge of Hegel's philosophy, obtained from his university professors, the Danish Hegelians Heiberg and Martensen. But it also betrays clear traces of the influence of Möller and Sibbern, Danish anti-Hegelians. Nils Tulstrup, a student of Kierkegaard's literary heritage, was correct in stating that even at that time Kierkegaard was no Hegelian. (cf. 68, 315) Within two weeks after the break he went to Berlin to hear Schelling's lectures. When he returned home after four months in Prussia, a new phase of his life began – creative seclusion.

Sören's father died in 1838. His mother, all his sisters and two brothers had died previously. Only one older brother, later a bishop, was left alive. It is no wonder that a critical article of Kierkegaard's on a novel by Hans Christian Andersen was entitled, "From the Papers of One Still Alive." His father left him a large amount of money, over 30 thousand rigsdalers in securities, which not only assured him a comfortable, even extravagant income to the end of his life but also enabled him to pay for publishing all his works. Sören settled down in a large house, with a secretary and housekeeper, and did not deny himself good cigars or fine wines. He lived an isolated life, in complete solitude. "I live in my room," he wrote in his *Diary*, "as if under siege, not wishing to see anyone and in constant fear of an attack by the enemy, i.e. some visit, and not wishing to go out." (8, 90) But every day he went out for a walk in the streets of Copenhagen, gaunt, bespectacled, with his "faithful friend," his umbrella, under his arm, in a broad-brimmed beaver hat and a cigar in his teeth, exchanging ironical greetings with acquaintances he met.

Upon returning to his "besieged fortress" he went to work. Except for a few months of teaching Latin and a short period of service in a seminary for ministers, Kierkegaard never had a job anywhere. His father had destined him for the ministry but he did not avail himself of his graduation from the theological faculty. And though in the early stages of his life he had the intention of becoming a village pastor, he never did so. He did not take advantage of the possibility of university work which was opened to him by his academic degree.

But his capacity for work was amazing! His literary fecundity is improbable. Standing at his desk, he wrote and wrote, day and night, by candlelight till dawn. "That is why I love you, silence of the hour of the spirit, here in my room, where no noise and no human voice break into the infinity of reflections and thoughts.... That is why I love you, quiet of solitude." (6, 15, 353–354)

In 1843 Kierkegaard's major work appeared, an ethico-esthetic book of 838 pages in two volumes, entitled *Either-Or*. Over the following twelve years (up to his death) he published more than six thousand printed pages (fifteen solid volumes in the collected works), and the papers he left unpublished come to almost ten thousand pages (including the *Diary*, which he started in 1838; and continued till the end of his life), filling twenty printed volumes. They are esthetic, ethical, religious (88 *Edifying Discourses*!), philosophical works. In this respect too the "Danish Socrates," as his admirers like to call him, differed radically from his prototype in ancient Greece who, as we know, did not write a line. His entire life was an idiosyncratic intoxication with literary creation. He compared himself to Scheherazade, who saved her life by tales, i.e. creation.

But there was no rest. *Either-Or* was successful (a second edition appeared in 1849), and Kierkegaard became a local celebrity, for it was no secret to anyone who was behind the pseudonym of Viktor Eremita and the other pseudonyms his affixed to his books as they appeared one after the other. But his breaking with Regina Olsen, especially after it was given literary expression in *Repetitions, Diary of a Seducer, Guilty? Not Guilty?*, aroused the animosity of the townspeople, endless gossip and finally a town scandal. *Korsar*, the satirical periodical (with a large circulation for the Copenhagen of those days, three thousand) continually mocked and caricatured Kierkegaard. "I am a martyr to ridicule," he wrote in his *Diary* (7, 360) On the streets of Copenhagen Kierkegaard was haunted by the abuse of passers-by. Boys ran after him shouting "Either-or" and threw stones at him. His seclusion and loneliness became even deeper. "If Copenhagen was ever of one opinion about anybody, I must say that it was unanimous about me: I am a parasite, an idler, a loafer, a cipher...." (6, 33, 56) "For an entire stratum of the population I actually exist as a kind of half-lunatic." (7, 591) Kierkegaard's diary is full of entries complaining that nobody, not a single person, understood him.

Throughout his life Kierkegaard regarded himself as an unhappy man. He was plagued by melancholy and hypochondria, interspersed with paroxysms of creative inspiration. "In the deepest sense I am an unhappy man, someone condemned from his earliest days to suffering bordering on insanity...." (7, 228) "Who am I? How did I happen to come into the world? Why was I not asked about it beforehand?...." (6, V–VI, 71) "Somewhere in England," Kierkegaard wrote, "there is a gravestone on which only one word is carved: 'The unhappiest.' I can imagine that someone will read that and reflect that no one is buried there and that the grave is destined for me." (7, 133)

Many articles, chapters of monographs and entire books have been written about Kierkegaard's psychopathology. The subject has been treated in a multiplicity of studies by psychiatrists and psychoanalysts. For all the divergences in their diagnoses they are all agreed that this was a psychically sick man. Even in his youth, he complained to his physician "of a disproportion in his nature between the physical and the psychic."

Specialists (in quotes and without quotes) have found every possible abnormality in the Danish philosopher (cf. 50): schizophrenia, epilepsy, the Oedipus complex, masochism, Narcissism, subconscious homosexuality, and most frequently of all, manic-depressive psychosis. This last was the diagnosis supported by the well-known Danish psychiatrist H. Hellweg. In all probability, that was the case. Sören Kierkegaard was a very strange unbalanced, queer, eccentric man. "Everything that exists frightens me," he admitted. "From the tiniest fly to the mystery of incarnation, everything is inexplicable to me, and especially I myself. My suffering is incredible, unlimited...." (8, 91) This is the confession of a twenty-five year old student living a dissipated life. "A unity of melancholy, reflection, fear of God, that unity is my essence." (7, 467)

It is impossible, impermissible, to ignore these facts in judging Kierkegaard's work; it is impossible not to take into account his melancholy, his depression, his mania, to subject them to a Husserlian epoché. But is it possible to reduce to these factors all the content in ideas of his work, his entire Weltanschauung? Is it possible, without denying the "intimate connection between his literary activity and his personal life" to agree unqualifiedly with Thompson that since Kierkegaard "was a very sick man," "the nature of his illness defines the primary perspective for understanding his works"? (93, p. XIII; retrans. from the Russian) that a manic-depressive psychosis is the key to his entire Weltanschauung? Or to agree with Mesnard as to "the absolute necessity of applying psychoanalysis to the entire philosophy of existence"? (79, 33) M. Grimault is correct in holding that "attempts to explain Kierkegaard's convictions exclusively by complexes and obsession...is an enterprise doomed to failure." (50, 119) No matter how closely all of Kierkegaard's work was interwoven with his personality, the content of his philosophy in ideas and theory, and its practical historical influence, are incomparably more significant and deserve more serious study than his individual eccentricities and morbid vagaries. His religious-philosophical doctrine requires careful study of its nature and social function rather than delving into the intimate details of his biography, no matter how entertaining.

Whatever our attitude towards the content in ideas of Kierkegaard's views and their philosophical value may be, it must be recognized that he was a man of a powerful mind and exceptional literary gifts. Artistic images, metaphors, accurate psychological analysis, irony now bitter and then biting and sarcastic, poetic fancy, agitation, tormented meditation, the lofty pathos of the preacher, and scornful denunciation – all these flowed freely from Kierkegaard's pen, all these means were skillfully used to affect the reader and convey to him the author's convictions and beliefs. Not only the diaries but all of Kierkegaard's literary production – esthetic, philosophical or religious – are introverted, directed inward on themselves, on personal feelings, refracted through the prism of his internal world. They are like volcanic eruptions of seething self-analysis and self-torment. "It would seem that I write things that should make stones sob," Kierkegaard wrote in his *Diary* (7, 311) "but they only make my contemporaries laugh." His ideas were certainly foreign to common sense and good judgment.

It is very characteristic of Kierkegaard's literary manner that he published all his fundamental works from *Either–Or* on (except the religious preachments of the *Edifying Discourses*) under a variety of pseudonyms, sometimes antithetical (Klimakus* and Anti-Klimakus). The purpose was not at all to conceal his authorship. In his capacity as "author of authors" he twists around, as it were, showing himself from various sides, in various roles, transforming himself and modelling various aspects and facets of his moods and feelings. In addition, as if the pseudonyms were not enough for him, he sometimes constructed his works "box into box" as his biographer puts it (58, 149), on several levels. Thus, in *Either–Or* the author's name is given as Viktor Eremita, who published papers A and papers B of Assessor Wilhelm, but A publishes papers he has discovered by the author of the *Diary of a Seducer*. These literary constructions were well termed "a marionette theater." (94, 18) In the wings, holding the strings of the marionettes, is the invisible "Individual," Sören Kierkegaard.

There are many characters in his puppet show but only one actor, and he is also the director and writes the scenarios. The scene is set by the rungs of a ladder leading the soul to heaven. For all the diversity of characters and genres that Kierkegaard employs, the basic trend of his works is one and the same – religious Christian fanaticism. For all the variety of form of his literary words, for all the diversification of their modulations, their tendency remains unaltered. "It often seems as if

---

* John Climacus (from the Greek *klimax*, ladder) was the abbot of a monastery in the Sinai in the VI century, a mystic who described the thirty rungs of the ladder that the soul climbs on the way to heaven. (6, 10, 190)

Kierkegaard did not write different books at all, but only rewrote the same book in different ways." (93, 164; retrans. from the Russian)

Despite the eternal doubts that haunted Kierkegaard, there was one thing he never doubted: that he was a genius. "I know very well," he said at the very outset of his literary career, "that right now I am the most gifted mind among all the youth...." (7, 164) And five years later: "That I am a writer who certainly honors Denmark is firmly established...." (7, 315) And again a year later: "O, after my death *Fear and Trembling* alone will suffice to make my name immortal." (7, 409) And in his posthumous *Views of My Literary Work* we have: "Although it was not given to my time to understand me, all the same I will belong to history...." (6, 33, 91)

And such was the case. His contemporaries rejected him. Neglect and even contempt were his lot all his life. "The wise gossips think I am crazy...." (Cited in 89, 124) His principal philosophical work, *Concluding Unscientific Postscript*, did not arouse the slightest interest and appeared in an edition of 50 copies. As for the *Philosophical Sketches* to which this work was an extensive commentary, "without any dispute, without the spilling of any blood or any ink, this work remained unnoticed, not reviewed anywhere, not mentioned anywhere...", he tells us (6, 16, I, 3) What role Kierkegaard's doctrine played in the history of philosophy thereafter is a question we shall return to after acquainting ourselves with the essence of the doctrine.

The last years of his life were marked by an irrepressible rebellion of this religious fanatic against the Protestant church of his time, against the attitudes and customs prevailing in it, its religious hypocrisy and formal ritual. In the pages of *Moment*, the militantly anti-clerical paper that he began with the last money remaining from his father's estate, Kierkegaard indignantly attacked the official institutions of the church and its guardians who had betrayed the precepts of Jesus Christ. The head of the Danish church was hit especially hard. The clericals were furious. The tenth and last number prepared by Kierkegaard did not appear. His enormous nervous agitation took its toll. Kierkegaard fell unconscious in the street and after a few days, refusing the sacraments, died at the age of forty-two. The date was November 11, 1855. He had chosen his epitaph long before his death: "He was an individual" *(hiin Enkelte)*. (6, 33, 113)

CHAPTER III

ANTI-HEGEL

Idealist philosophy reached its apogee in Hegel's *Science of Logic*. Here philosophical rationalism, in its idealist refraction, took on its perfected form as panlogism: "Being is thought." (16, 4, 29) What is not rational has no reality. For all the basic divergence of Hegelian rationalism from the philosophy of enlightenment of the pre-revolutionary French bourgeoisie, they have in common the cult of reason. For Hegel, "faith in the power of reason is the first condition of philosophical studies.... The secret essence of the Universe has no power within it that could oppose the intrepidity of knowledge..." (16, 1, 16) "The words inscribed on the veil of Isis: 'I am that which was, is and will be; no mortal has lifted my veil,' vanish before the power of thought." (16, 2, 15) Knowledge is the self-knowledge of being as thinking. It can not be anything other than logical knowledge. But that in turn is the only trustworthy scientific knowledge. "...What is best in the philosophy of our time considers its value to consist in its scientific character... in point of fact it only becomes significant thanks to its scientific character." (16, 4, 39)

The great historical achievement of Hegel, the basis of the superiority of the "rational idealism" he worked out over the form of materialism contemporary with him is that his rationalism, while idealist, is yet a *dialectical* rationalism, an historically new stage in the development of theoretical thinking, an historically new form of logic – dialectical logic.

At the same time, his *objective* logic, the logic of things, the logic of the self-development of objective reality, shrouds actual reality in a dense idealist cloud. The veil of Isis is replaced by a veil of absolute idealism. Dialectics takes on the incorporeal character of the self-movement of concepts, while depriving nature, as "other-being of the spirit," of self-movement.

Hegel's formula, "Everything real is rational," means not only that it is accessible to reason and only to reason; the formula hypostatizes reason and underpins objective reality with the "world spirit," the "absolute idea" – the objectified projection of logical thinking, thereby giving all dialectical categories a mystified character.

Yet the formula of the reasonableness of reality is ambiguous: Although Hegel distinguishes between "reality" and "existence," and the formula thereby permits of a progressive interpretation, the conclusions of Hegel's system reveal the inconsequence of his dialectics, its conservative limitations, its justification of and apology for what exists, Hegel's system falls into contradiction with the dialectical method, becomes a brake on further development, paralyzes prospects for forward movement, gives dialectics a retrospective character, depriving it of its revolutionary tendency. Hegel's dialectics is not limited to the sphere of the possible, as the late Schelling insisted, and does not preclude rational knowledge of reality, but it impedes understanding of the real possibility of unlimited innovation and development that is latent in reality at any of its stages.

At the same time, the meta-empirical method of Hegelian logic had a positive side: the desire to arrive at the logical structure of universal law through the empirical diversity of the particular and accidental. The dialectical method, like Röntgen rays, aims at the logical framework of all process.

In Hegel's philosophy philosophical idealism gave everything it was capable of giving, and that was a great deal. That is why criticism of Hegel's doctrine, in a different way, but to the same extent as criticism of the founder of German classical idealism, proved to be possible from the right or the left, as criticism of the "rational core" of the doctrine and as criticism of what prevented the "rational core" from putting out rational shoots.

When I speak of criticism of Hegel from the right and the left, I have in mind here not the clash of the opposing right and left Hegelian interpretations of Hegel but rather anti-Hegelianism: on one side Feuerbach, from a materialist position, and on the other Kierkegaard in the idealist camp, from the position of a different form of idealism radically different from Hegel's.

For Kierkegaard, Hegel is the culminating point of the development of philosophy, in which reason, that "idol" of Western contemplative thought, reached its apex. For him, Hegel is The Philosopher. "All of S. Kierkegaard's thinking should be regarded as a revolt against Hegel's thinking." (47, 91) His entire doctrine is pointed against the "cult" of Hegel, against those for whom "the Hegelian philosophy, supported by all-powerful public opinion, is thought of as a philosophy standing at the high point of all possible science; a philosophy outside of which there is no salvation, only darkness and stupidity." (6, 36, 108) All of Kierkegaard's doctrine is the antithesis of the rationalism, objectivism, scientific character embodied in Hegel's philosophy. The Hegelian panlogism is "the spiritual antipodes" of Kierkegaard. (43, 109) His entire doctrine is militant anti-Hegelianism, hostility to the tendencies broadly developed in classical German philosophy and culminating in the *Science of Logic*, in logic understood as the science of sciences.

In Kierkegaard's words, "Despite Hegel's remarkable merits and colossal learning, his achievements constantly remind us that he was a professor of philosophy in the higher style of the German spirit, for he will explain anything you please, cost what it may." (6, 11–12, 17) "Hegel was a philosophy professor, not a thinker," he writes. (7, 448) Kierkegaard is roused to wrath by "the accursed dishonesty that Hegel introduced into philosophy." (7, 185) The entire structure of Hegel's thought, the whole spirit of his doctrine are insufferable to the anti-Hegelian of Copenhagen. He has contempt for Hegel's Danish supporters, Heiberg and Martensen.

Kierkegaard makes a frontal attack on the system of Hegel, rejecting the very idea of constructing a philosophical system as something complete and finished. He declares: "A system of being is impossible.... System and completeness correspond to one another; but being is the direct opposite to that," (6, 16, I, 111) and makes a call to go *"back* from system" (6, 33, 50); in so doing he hits at a real defect in Hegel's philosophy, in which the system fetters consistent development of the dialectical method. He further condemns the Hegelian dialectic for having a retrospective character and being able "to understand only what has happened, been completed," as a result of which "what is said in Hegel about process and becoming becomes illusory." (6, 16, II, 7) For him Hegel is a prophet facing towards the past. But what is involved here is not at all a desire to eliminate the inconsistencies of the Hegelian dialectic but an attack on dialectical logic as the highest form of objective rational knowledge. Kierkegaard rejects Hegelianism as a contemplative philosophy, and proclaims: "...I came into the world and my calling was to counteract speculation, and that is my real task...." (6, 16, I, 225) Hegel's *system* is criticized by Kierkegaard, not for the sake of reinforcing and developing the dialectical *method* but for the sake of eliminating the new and fruitful things with which the genius who was the author of dialectical logic enriched philosophical thought. The weak points of Hegel's philosophy are utilized in order to reject everything that was healthy and permanent in it.

In Kierkegaard the critique of the Hegelian philosophical system as the end of philosophical development, as a limitation of Hegel's own dialectical method turns into a critique of systematic philosophy in general, of philosophy as a construction of a theoretical system. But doesn't he himself set up against Hegel a system of his own of opinions and convictions, however unsystematically that system may have been set forth in his expressionistic works?

Nils Tulstrup, an ardent admirer of Kierkegaard, is correct in stating that from the outset of his theoretical activity, even as early as his dissertation, Kierkegaard was an anti-Hegelian, completely at variance with Hegel's philosophical doctrine. And even in the cases where he used an indirect method for criticizing Hegel, by suggestion, he was like a wolf in sheep's clothing. (cf. 68, 315–316) Actually, the critique of Hegel's system was by no means the only aim of his polemic. He rejected Hegel's philosophy altogether, as a whole. His entire doctrine, regarded on the negative plane, was a frontal attack on all of the philosophical tradition whose foundation was laid by Descartes and whose apotheosis was Hegel, the tradition of philosophical rationalism. From this point of view, "Kierkegaard's polemic against Hegel is the classical philosophical and ideological polemic of the nineteenth century." (34, 7)

Kierkegaard's militant anti-Hegelianism remains within the limits of a conflict inside the idealist camp. His categorical rejection of the Hegelian identity of being and thought is not for the reason that it is idealist but because Hegel's idealist conception of being identifies the spiritual principle with logical thinking, makes logicalness an immanent attribute of being, regards being as logical by its very nature. Hegel's basic argument, according to Kierkegaard, does not explain what being is; his formula is tautological, since in him "thought and being signify one and the same thing." (6, 16, I, 180) When Kierkegaard declares that "the identity of thinking and being is a chimera of abstraction," (6, 16, I, 187) he aims at refuting not idealism but rationalism. For him, being does not cease to be spiritual, it ceases to be rational, capable of being expressed in logical determinations, accessible to logical thought.

The chasm separating Hegel's idealist philosophy and Kierkegaard's idealist philosophy (or rather, as Sartre puts it, anti-philosophy) is the view of the relationship between dialectics and logic. While Hegel raised logic to the level of dialectics, confirming their unity, their identity, since for him dialectics is exactly logic, Kierkegaard set it as his task and his calling to put them apart. His entire philosophical doctrine is permeated with the conviction that dialectics is incompatible with logic, that they are antinomies. For Kierkegaard, what is logical is not dialectical and what is dialectical is not logical.

Kierkegaard rejects "Hegel's much-trumpeted discovery, introducing movement into logic...a discovery which means, to be exact, the confusion of logic. And it is very strange to take movement as the basis of the sphere in which movement is unthinkable; or to try to explain movement by logic, when in fact logic is unable to explain movement." (6, 16, I, 102) "In logic," Kierkegaard says, "no movement of any kind can *come into being*, since logic *is* and everything logical merely *is*...."

(6, 11–12, 9) It does not follow from this, by any means, that Kierkegaard sets himself the task of rehabilitating formal-metaphysical logic as the only acceptable and reliable philosophical method, the "organon." Not at all. His aim is to justify alogism.

It may appear that in Kierkegaard there are the Eleatic themes of negative dialectics, the impossibility of expressing movement in the logic of concepts which fix what is transitory, ossify what is living. Actually, the aim here is something diametrically opposite to that of the Eleatics: whereas for the Eleatics the rational, the logical, is the criterion of what is true and entails denial of objective dialectics, for Kierkegaard the rational, the logical, is groundless, "impotent," untrue, just because no logic is able to express movement. He holds that it is impossible to resolve the problem posed by Hegel: to set up a logic that would be able to do what was unattainable to the earlier logic, a logic capable of expressing the movement of being in the movement of its concepts. He calls the project of "introducing into logic contradiction, movement, transition, etc." "eyewash." (6, 16, II, 5) Kierkegaard inverts Zeno's paradox: instead of denying movement on the ground that it has been proved to be contradictory, he rejects reason on the ground that motion has been proved to contain an internal contradiction. (cf. 44, 16) For Kierkegaard as for Zeno: either logic or movement; but the Eleatics contraposed rational knowledge to movement, while Kierkegaard contraposes movement to rational knowledge. "The eternal expression of logic is something that the Eleatics, by a misunderstanding, transferred to existence: nothing becomes, everything is." (6, 11–12, 9) As we shall see, Kierkegaard does not deal with becoming as immanent in objective reality, and not even with the formation of thought itself, that is, with movement in the sense of either objective or subjective dialectics.

Nonetheless, Kierkegaard is a champion of dialectics. "I am a born dialectician by nature," he writes. (6, 33, 150) He regards all his literary activity as "dialectical from beginning to end." (6, 33, 29) We find a statement like the following: "...All of me is solid dialectics." (9, 2, 82) But his "dialectics" is incompatible, not only with Hegel's system but also with Hegel's dialectical method. "The absolute method invented by Hegel," says Kierkegaard, "is a dubious matter even in logic, really a brilliant tautology; that method, by means of all sorts of subterfuges and thaumaturgic tricks, came to the rescue of *scientific prejudices*." (6, 10, 74)

The overwhelming majority of Kierkegaard specialists (including those who are not proponents of existentialism) regard Kierkegaard as a true dialectician. Anna Paulsen characterizes Kierkegaard as "a dialectician to a high degree." (85, 432) For W. Anz, "Kierkegaard and Hegel are both dialecticians." (29, 70) I. Bogen asserts that "Kierkegaard employed the 'dialectical' method in the Hegelian sense." (38, 383) Even more, in his opinion "Kierkegaard was a rationalist in precisely the same sense as Hegel." (38, 374) The fascizing Nietzschean Beimler went so far as to hold that Kierkegaard surpassed Hegel in consistent application of the dialectical method. We trust that the last example will convince the reader of how far these statements are from objective truth. Our key to resolution of the problem of Kierkegaard's "dialectics" will be Lenin's principle of the indissoluble unity of logic and dialectics.

Kierkegaard professes to develop an anti-Hegelian dialectics, one derived from Socrates. There is current among us a characterization of Hegel's dialectics as "the second historical form of dialectics." But even an elementary acquaintance with the history of ancient philosophy will show that there were in it not one but two different forms of dialectics (abstracting from the Eleatic doctrine, which Hegel too describes as not an anti-dialectics but a particular kind of "subjective dialectics"): Heraclitus' objective primitive-materialist dialectics of being, and Socrates' subjective idealist dialectics of knowledge. Hegel's dialectics, as the culmination of classical German idealism, is the third historical form of dialectics, and rises to an incomparably higher level. Hegel is both right and wrong in saying that "there is not a single proposition of Heraclitus that I did not adopt in my Logic," (16, 12, 246) for in taking over, developing and deepening Heraclitus's dialectics he deprived it of its materialist essence. At the same time, Hegel's subjectivistic logic is inseparably linked to his objective logic, and thereby differs essentially from the Socratic dialectic, being richer, more diversified and deeper. The idealistically elaborated objective dialectic is synthesized with the objectively based subjective dialectic as method and theory of knowledge. Kierkegaard justly termed it "absolute dialectics." That is why a high valuation of Heraclitean dialectics: "Here new land is opened to us" (16, 9, 246) is combined in Hegel with an equally high valuation of Socratic dialectics: "On the whole, Socrates is a great turning point in history." (16, 10, 88)

Kierkegaard rejects Hegel's dialectical method and counterposes the Socratic dialectic to it: "...in any event it is certain that he (Hegel) has absolutely nothing in common with Socrates." (6, 16, II, 63) Attacking Hegel's doctrine and belittling it in every way, Kierkegaard goes into raptures over Socrates, whom he calls his teacher. (6, 33, 48) "The only one who consoles me is Socrates." (6, 16, I, 152) "O, old Socrates, greatest of all people," he exclaims. (7, 457) "Outside of Christianity you, Socrates, are the one and only, the noble, straightforward sage: you were the real reformer." (7, 598) "...You are the one and only *man*, whom

I rejoice to recognize as a thinker...", he wrote just before his death. (6, 34, 329)

What is it in Socrates that attracts Kierkegaard, and what in Hegel repels him? Above all, the conception of the object of philosophy, the breach with the entire Ionian line of development, from Thales to Democritus, with philosophy as a striving for a scientific understanding of the world. Breaking with philosophy as with knowledge of the objective world, Socrates "was not interested either in world history nor in astronomy..." (6, 16, I, 75); he turned philosophy from the object to the subject, inward, reducing it to knowledge of the self, not of the world. Socratism is "subjectivism in its second stage;" (7, 628) "for the Socratic way of thinking every person is a center for himself, and all the world revolves centripetally around him...." (6, 10, 9)

Kierkegaard is attracted by Socrates' "maieutic" dialectics, a method Socrates adapted from his mother's art as midwife, a method furthering the birth of truth in dialogued search for it, in doubt and dispute, in a questioning approach to what is not known, in a word, subjective dialectics, the art of asking oneself about oneself.

From the beginning of his activity, in his master's dissertation, Kierkegaard was attracted by Socratic irony, which Hegel defined as "only the subjective form of dialectics," whose function is "to instill in people doubt of their own presuppositions, while "dialectics in the true sense deals with the bases of the object being considered." (16, 10, 45) Kierkegaard extols Socrates in that he "brought irony into the world and gave that name to his own creation," (6, 10, 136), making wide use in his works of ironical reflection as a method of self-knowledge.

In point of fact Kierkegaard's "dialectics" was not a reproduction of the Socratic dialectic. It is not only that Kierkegaard himself distinguished his "dialectics" from the Socratic as a new and more perfect form of it, *Christian* Socraticism. His *Philosophical Sketches* end in a contraposition of his method to the Socratic, concluding with the ironical phrase: "But when one wants to go beyond Socrates and yet say the same thing as he did, but far from it as well, then that at least is not Socratic." (6, 10, 107)

The difference between Kierkegaard's Christian neo-Socraticism from the historical (or rather, the Platonized) Socraticism is far deeper than Kierkegaard supposes. Kierkegaard's method differs from that of Socrates in its essence. The divide between the two is constituted by Socrates' logical rationalism, which is incompatible with Kierkegaard's views. Although "Socrates' principle... is that man must find both the goal of his actions and the final goal of the world, starting only from himself, and reach the truth by his own powers," still, according to Socrates, "correct thinking thinks in such a way that its content is yet not subjective but objective." (16, 10, 35) Kierkegaard himself realizes this, and observes in his *Diary* that Socrates "relates with objectivity to his own subjectivity." (7, 628) The Socratic ethics, which is the foundation of his method, is rationalistic, not only in its criteria but in its guarantee – rational self-knowledge. In it, virtue appears as a function of reason. Kierkegaard's ethical construct (and Kierkegaardianism, like Socraticism, is primarily an ethical doctrine) is based on his *method*, directly contraverting Socrates's rationalism. In Socrates maieutics and irony are a means towards ascertaining objective truth, Kierkegaard employs them to obtain subjective truth, "the truth for me," since he does not recognize any other truth: "...objectively there is no truth...." (6, 16, I, 69) Kierkegaard strongly opposes the acception of truth as knowledge. "In our time," he states, "it is believed, apparently, that knowledge gives superiority and that if one only achieves knowledge of the truth, that can help any one." (6, 16, I, 294) As he sees it, objective knowledge is not a guide to action, directions for conduct. "In existence, the domination of thinking leads only to error." (6, 16, II, 51) This is why the title of "Danish Socrates" so often applied in the apologetic literature on Kierkegaard has little justification in comparison to the rationalist inspiration of the Athenian sage.

The aspiration to objective scientific knowledge is, Kierkegaard says, "the misfortune of our time," (6, 16, I, 253) and must be done away with at all costs. To the dialectical unity of the subjective and the objective he contraposes their disjunction: "Objective thinking has no relation whatever to existing subjectivity." (6, 16, I, 116) Divorcing the subjective from the objective, Kierkegaard blames contemplative philosophy for ignoring the subjective in its absorption with the objective: "Speculative (philosophers) in our times are so stupidly objective that they forget entirely that the thinking person himself is at the same time the musical instrument, the flute, on which they are playing.... Objective thinking is not concerned at all with the thinker...." (7, 190–191) The way to objective truth leads away from the subject, turns its back on him, gives him nothing, treats the subject with proud disdain. That is why for the subject, for the existing person, pure thought is a worthless 'chimera.' (6, 16, II, 11)

Discarding objective knowledge from the outset and denying it any significance or actuality, Kierkegaard calls on us to take the directly contrary path, that of radical subjectivism. "I demand nothing other than recognition that in our *objective* times I am the only one incapable of being objective." (6, 16, I, 278) This absolute contraposition of subjectivity and objectivity is the cornerstone of his entire philosophy, whose first task is to overthrow "the false idea of knowledge and its results that those people have who speak of objective results, not realizing that it is precisely the genuine philosopher who is, in the highest degree, subjective." (7, 50)

Kierkegaard, attacking the Hegelian *method*, does not allow a dialectics that aims at objective scientific knowledge. He regards *objective* dialectics as unattainable. He indignantly cites Hegel's words in the *Phenomenology of Spirit* to the effect that movement and development take place "behind the back of consciousness." In essence, the denial of objective dialectics goes beyond the framework of a critique of the method of *idealist* dialectics. Kierkegaard's unwearying polemic against objective dialectics as a method aiming at arriving at rational, objective, scientific knowledge excludes even more the materialist reworking of it that *in fact* is the realization of such knowledge. When E. Geismar asserts that Kierkegaard's central arguments against Hegel "have triumphant power against modern naturalism as well," (45, 252) he takes his desire for actuality, but he is right in this repect, that these arguments are directed against every objective dialectics, both idealist and "naturalist."

Incidentally, accusing Hegel of one-sided objectivism, ignoring subjectivity, does not correspond to Hegel's actual doctrine. The absolute idea, understood, for all its objectivity, as a self-moving, active, dynamic first principle, is also, for Hegel, the subject of development. At the same time, spirit as the highest stage of this development signifies the attainment of subjectivity the absolute idea in the exact sense of the term, as self-knowledge.

However, Kierkegaard's critique of objective idealism from the position of subjective idealism is not a reason for identifying his doctrine with such forms of subjective idealism as Berkeleyanism, or still less Fichteanism. His is a particular, specific form of subjectivism, breaking with the conception of the subject as a knowing, thinking being, taking it "not in the abstract sense in which Fichte took the word...." (6, 11–12, 140) *Sum cogitans* (I think) is not a Kierkegaardian first principle. For him "to be" is also not *percipi* (be perceived). Perceptibility is just as unacceptable a basis for his philosophy as thinking is. "Sensory trustworthiness is an error... historical knowledge is deception of the senses... and the speculative result is an illusion." (6, 16, I, 73) "To be" is "to exist," which for Kierkegaard means to feel, to experience, to go through, to suffer, to strive. "Genuine subjectivity is not intellectual subjectivity... but ethically existing subjectivity." (6, 16, I, 17) "My main idea," he writes in his fundamental philosophical work, *Concluding Unscientific Postscript*, "was that in our days people have forgotten, because of the abundance of knowledge, what it means to 'exist' and what inwardness

(Inderlighed, Innerlichkeit) means...."* (6, 16, I, 242) Subjectivism is contraposed to objective knowledge, not as a principle of knowledge but as inclination, passion. "Passion is what subjectivity is, and with an objective approach there is none." (6, 16, I, 120)

Subjectivity understood in an emotional-voluntaristic sense is, for Kierkegaard, what real actuality is, and it excludes objective reality from the sphere of philosophy. "Subjectivity is actuality." (6, 16, II, 47) For this form of subjective idealism "spirit is inwardness, inwardness is subjectivity, subjectivity is essentially passion...." (6, 16, I, 28) And for each subject his own existence is *his* actuality. "The individual's own ethical actuality is the only actuality." (6, 16, II, 29)

This discloses the inner sense of Kierkegaard's critique of the Hegelian identity of thought and being. It is denied not as an idealistic but as a rationalistic first principle: actuality cannot be identified with thought, inasmuch as it is not thinkable. "The only thing, in itself, that does not admit of thought of it is existence, with which thought has nothing in common." (6, 16, II, 31) But there is no place in Kierkegaard's philosophy for any other being-in-itself; for him, identification of the actual with the true is only "Hegelian chatter." (7, 630) "Oh that Hegel!... How the gods laughed! What a despicable professor, seeing far and wide the necessity of all things...." (7, 604)

Dissociating himself vigorously from the Hegelian dialectic as the logic of being and thought, Kierkegaard advances, in opposition to him, his own subjective-idealist "dialectics," which has no connection with logic, an existential "dialectics of existence" in the emotional – voluntaristic sense that Kierkegaard puts into the concept of "existence."

None of Kierkegaard's adherents doubts the dialectical nature of his philosophy. Is not the category of "becoming" decisive for Kierkegaardian thought? Are not movement, transition, leaps, concepts of primary importance for him? (cf. 63, 35) The relentless battle against the Hegelian dialectical method is said to be nothing other than the establishment of another, new form of dialectics, not only different but directly contrary to the Hegelian. For example, A. Cortese writes: "Kierkegaard's dialectics was different as compared to Hegel's." (67, 5, 129) In the words of R. Heiss, "Kierkegaard desires to give dialectical thought an entirely different direction and significance." (55, 201) What then was the basic difference of Kierkegaard's "new dialectics" from the dialectics of Hegel which it had overcome? Primarily in that the existential dialectics is inaccessible to logical thinking. It does not fit in the Procrustean bed of *any* logic. For Kierkegaard, a thinkable dialectics is impassive, bookish

---

* Directedness inward towards oneself. "Self-observation," "introspection" do not reproduce the shade of meaning that Kierkegaard gives this favorite term of his.

dialectics, not a vital one; subjectivist dialectics knows no laws; it is not subject to logical coordination and systematization. "To exist" is possible only "dialectically." "Subjectivity...always has dialectics within itself...." (6, 16, I, 31) Becoming, contradictions, leaps are inseparable from subjectivity, which knows no rest and cannot be expressed in static conceptual categories. "Existence is unthinkable without movement." (6, il, II, 9) "And if he exists, then is he not in the process of becoming?" (6, 16, II, 6) "...Wherever there is life, there also is contradiction." (6, 16, II, 9) But all these dialectical-sounding categories undergo strange alterations in the subjectivist "dialectics."

Kierkegaard regards the Hegelian dialectics as being not only objective but also "quantitative." He constantly contrasts to it his own dialectics as "qualitative," in which the transition to the new and different takes place by leaps. How baseless it is to define as "quantitative dialectics" the Hegelian law of the passage of quantity into quality will be obvious to anyone who has even the slightest notion of that law. For, its essence is precisely the identity of these categorial opposites in the process of development. Kierkegaard calls it "a superstition, when it is supposed in logic that a new quality arises by way of continued quantitative determination." (6, 11–12, 27) He denies the significance of the quantitative stage as prerequisite of the arisal of the new quality. He holds that "Higher quantitative determination explains a leap just as little as does lower quantitative determination." (6, 11–12, 36) Asserting that "the new arises in the form of leaps," (6, 11–12, 86) Kierkegaard thereby denies the element of continuity conserved in the transition to the new. The leap, according to Kierkegaard, is not a necessity, not even if it is a question of logical necessity. Hegel wants to explain the leap, Kierkegaard says, but it is impossible to explain, it is inexplicable, it excludes any kind of "mediation." The new quality appears "with the suddenness of the mysterious." (6, 11–12, 28) Even though Hegel recognizes leaps, he gives the concept a logical meaning. "The trouble with Hegel is that he wants to give meaning to the leap and at the same time does not want to, inasmuch as he wants to do it within the limits of logic." (6, 11–12, 28) For Kierkegaard, on the other hand, a leap is non-logical, inaccessible to rational understanding; it does not follow with logical necessity from the preceding state. A leap is sudden, inexplicable, irrational. Admitting preliminary quantitative changes as presuppositions of the leap introduces an element of necessity into its origin, endows it with a logical quality, and that is just why Kierkegaard rejects it. He repeats over and over again that a qualitative leap, by virtue of its very essence as a leap, is inaccessible to knowledge. A leap is what "no science has explained nor can explain." (6, 11–12, 61) For the passage from one qualitative state into another is a product not of necessity but of freedom. A discontinuous transition into something else is not a logical conclusion, not an inference, but a free choice, resoluteness, decision, achievement. And it is accomplished, not as a logical synthesis, not as "an Hegelian process of digestion in three stomachs: at first directly, then it is masticated again, then belched up again," (7, 61) but in anxiety, searchings, striving, hope, fear, despair. This is not a contemplative, speculative dialectics but, as Kierkegaard himself calls it, "pathetic dialectics."

An analogous transformation is applied to all the categories of rational dialectics, of dialectical logic into existential, pathetic "dialectics," whose postulate is the non-logical nature of movement. "The concept of movement...," says Kierkegaard, "cannot have any place in logic." (6, 11–12, 9)

Following Hegel, Kierkegaard defines becoming as passage from non-being to being. (6, 10, 69) But in Hegel, he holds, "negation, transition, mediation are three mummified, dubious secret agents setting everything in motion" (6, 11–12, 83), and not at all "uneasy heads" that are not subject to any logic. Becoming is change, a becoming other, passage into something else, passage from possibility to actuality. But, according to Kierkegaard, there is a basic qualitative difference between possibility and actuality. "...What an infinite difference there is between the understanding of anything in possibility and the understanding of the same thing in actuality," he says in his *Diary*. (7, 427) In contradistinction to possibility, actuality, in his opinion, cannot be the object of logical understanding. "Thinkable reality is possibility, and thinking should put aside all questions as to whether something is actual." (6, 16, II, 31)

Kierkegaard sees the main source of error in this question as incorrect understanding of the relationship between possibility and actuality to necessity. Becoming is not subject to necessity and incompatible with it. "Anything that becomes proves by its mere becoming that it is not necessary; for the only thing that cannot become is the necessary, since what is necessary is." (6, 10, 238) In this respect the actual is as alien to the necessary as the possible is: "The actual is no more necessary than the possible, for the necessary is absolutely different from both." (6, 10, 239) Aristotle's doctrine of the passage of possibility into actuality is untenable, Kierkegaard says, if for no other reason than that it starts from the assertion that everything necessary is possible, whereas actually both the possible, and the actual, and becoming as the passage from one to the other, have nothing to do with necessity and are incompatible with it. Since the passage of possibility into actuality is not accomplished under necessity but in freedom, "no becoming is a necessity." (6, 10, 239) "Becoming is a change in actuality, brought about by means of freedom,"

(6, 10, 241) since the final cause is always a freely acting cause. Kierkegaard applies this not only to the sphere of "existence," but also to the laws of nature, insofar as becoming is concerned. "I think," he wrote to Lund in 1835, "that nature itself may be considered from a point of view that does not require having recourse to the secrets of science." (6, 35, 5) Kierkegaard's entire analysis of becoming denies any objective regularity of development that is accessible to logical, scientific comprehension. "But I," he asserts, "thanks to qualitative dialectics, am readily persuaded that in the qualitative sense the Universe simply has not made a single step forward for a hundred thousand years...." (6, 17, 135)

Kierkegaard's reproaches to Hegel on the grounds that the Hegelian dialectic precludes freedom, and with it change, have no basis. The dialectical understanding of these categories consists precisely in the point that necessity and freedom, and necessity and chance, are linked by the unity of opposites and do not exclude one another. When Kierkegaard sets as his goal "the destruction of the concept of necessity" in the name of freedom and chance, he contraposes them metaphysically and thereby breaks with dialectics. Equally anti-dialectical is the divorce of actuality from possibility, which Kierkegaard upholds against Hegel's dialectical understanding of their interpenetration, which appears in the distinction of formal and real possibility.

Thus, Kierkegaard does not found a new form of dialectics different from the Hegelian; he breaks with dialectics. The relationship of quantity and quality, like the relationships of possibility and actuality, freedom and necessity, necessity and chance, are not dialectical in him, but dichotomous; for him, these categories are mutually exclusive. Equally metaphysical is his notion of the relationship of continuity and discreteness as absolute, unrelatable opposites. While in Hegel we have dialectical unity of opposites: quantity and quality, continuity and discreteness, renovation and historical succession; while in him the very *connection* of successive qualitative states is accomplished by means of discontinuous *breaks* and the line of development is the base line of measurements: in Kierkegaard there is contraposed to this dialectical logic a metaphysical pattern of alternatives which not only have nothing in common with dialectics but tend to break with logic altogether. But although he succeeded in breaking with dialectics, the break with logic proves to be inoperable, since in order to justify that break Kierkegaard was forced to apply every kind of logical effort and shift. For sophistry is still a kind of logic, even though an abuse of logic.

Kierkegaard's critique of the dialectical law of the passage of quantity into quality is a clear illustration of his relation to dialectics in general, since that law is one of the expressions of the universal dialectical principle: process as the unity of opposites in all the diversity of its phenomena. To this basic principle of dialectics Kierkegaard opposes a set of metaphysical dichotomies on the principle of either–or. This holds true for all the categories Kierkegaard considers. The category of contradiction runs through Kierkegaard's entire world view: "Wherever there is life there is contradiction." (6, 16, II, 223) But for him the invariant attribute of existence is not logical but pathetic contradiction. Passion is nothing but contradiction at its most tense. Where there is no life, no passion, there there is no contradiction. Outside of existence there is no contradiction, while existential contradiction itself does not presuppose unity, but expels, removes it. Moreover, contradiction, even in its existential interpretation, is not in Kierkegaard the motive force of development. "The word 'contradiction,' " he explains, "should not be taken here in the accursed sense that Hegel ascribes to it, imagining for himself and assuring others that it has creative power." (6, 10, 83)

An anti-dialectical approach is characteristic of all of existential "dialectics." Kierkegaard not only categorically excludes dialectics from logic, insisting that "in constructing a logical system it is necessary above all to make sure that nothing that is subject to the dialectics of being enters into it...." (6, 16, I, 101); but even in extralogical existence all the Kierkegaardian "dialectics" is illusory just because it predetermines an undialectical logic based on the introduction of *nec plus ultra* formal-logical antitheses which allow no synthetic "removal" of the "mediation" so hated by Kierkegaard. "...Mediation is the chimera that in Hegel is to explain everything...." (6, 4, 42) Absolute opposites, he declares, cannot be mediated. For him, negation excludes assertion, leaps–consequentiality, contradiction–unity, process–being, the concrete–the abstract, time–eternity, transformation–being governed by law, novelty–succession, possibility–actuality, freedom–necessity, necessity–chance, essence–existence, and so forth. His entire pseudo-dialectics is a palisade of dichotomies, absolute contrasts, incompatible and irreconcilable antagonisms, "the immortal either-or." "If I," Kierkegaard admits, "were a better dialectician than I am, I should still have one limit; and, in essence, unshakable devotion to the absolute and absolute distinctions – that is what makes a good dialectician." (6, 10, 105–106) Is it possible, after that, to speak of "existential dialectics" as a new historical form of dialectics, supplanting dialectical logic? To call things by their right names, "existential dialectics," for all its parade of process, contradiction, and leaps, and for all its attachment to Socratic irony and maieutics, means essentially a break with the historical development of dialectical thought, a leading of philosophy into the blind alley of metaphysical irrationalism.

Whereas Zeno's paradoxes and Kant's antinomies, leading right up to the limit of the logic of the *understanding*, brought philosophical thought to the threshold of a higher, *rational*, dialectical logic, Kierkegaard's "qualitative disjunction" (6, 16, II, 54) leads away in the opposite direction. When he reproaches Hegel for denying contradiction, his criticism is conducted from an anti-dialectical position which does not allow the unity of opposites. Jean Wahl said well on this matter that "Kierkegaard's thought is a cleaving sword: the internal is not the external, reason is not history, the subjective is not the objective, culture is not religion." (96, 131) But this kind of cleaving brings out most clearly the fact that his method is diametrically opposed to dialectics.

Kierkegaard's anti-dialectical quality appears just as markedly in his statement of the problem of historicism, two which he gave particular attention in the *Philosophical Sketches*.

In the historical sciences the Hegelian method, in Kierkegaard's words, takes on the character of an *idée fixe*; here, he says, the method assumes a concreteness that is untypical of Hegel, inasmuch as "history is the concretization of the Idea." (6, 10, 74) This, he grants, makes it possible for Hegel "to exhibit his unusual erudition" in historical learning, but that does not justify his method. The category of the "historical" demands a different approach and a different understanding.

Kierkegaard's fiercest attacks are made against the Hegelian dialectic of the historical and the logical; he asserts the alogical nature of the historical, excluding all necessity.

For Kierkegaard the historical is what has passed, what has become, what is completed and is as such unchanging, even though that unchangingness is the result of change. But does it follow from this that the past cannot *become* other, that it is necessary, i.e. could not be other? He answers in the negative: "...the past is not necessary by virtue of the fact that it has been; it did not become necessary thanks to its becoming...." (6, 10, 76) What Kierkegaard is driving at is to eliminate necessity from the historical as what has been completed (and not only as what has not yet been completed, is being completed). This is a criticism not of fatalism but of determinism, of historical lawfulness, which makes possible logical explanation and the application of "method," as Kierkegaard puts it.

He shares the opinion of Hegel (who thereby limited his dialectics) that nature has no history, since "nature is too abstract to be dialectical, in the strict sense, with respect to time." (6, 10, 72) Here abstractness is taken in the sense of absence of the possibilities which freedom opens up for becoming.

The denial of historical lawfulness is based by Kierkegaard precisely on the postulate that what has been is the result of free choice. "The past has already become; but becoming is change in actuality accomplished by means of freedom. If the past had happened of necessity, it would no longer belong to freedom and thus would not belong to that by means of which it came into being." (6, 10, 74) For Kierkegaard historical process in a function of "a cause acting absolutely freely." (6, 10, 72) Not being necessary, it is thereby alogical as well.

But no matter how great the importance that Kierkegaard attributes to denial of regularity, not only in the future but in the historical past, his treatment of the historical is conditioned primarily by the dichotomy of the historical as temporal and eternal, which is of the first importance in his entire conception. For him, the eternal is not unending time but what is outside of time, anti-time. "...All knowledge is either knowledge of the eternal, putting aside the temporal and historical as indifferent, or it is purely historical knowledge." (6, 10, 52) Here is one more of the alternatives so characteristic of Kierkegaard. "...the perfection of the eternal lies in that it has no history, and is the only thing that is and none the less has absolutely no history." (6, 10, 72) Thus, the ahistorical is admitted along with the historical and contrary to it and, of course, in the fact of the eternal the historical loses all significance, fades into the background. The center of interest is transferred from the transitory historical to the eternal as constant, non-transitory, innocent of novelty. "God does not exist, He is eternal." (6, 16, II, 35) Historical endlessness in time is but a "parody on eternity" (6, 11–12, 84), since the only function of time is to pass. "Life in time, and belonging only to time, is devoid of the real." (6, 11–12, 85) But the kingdom of the unchanging, eternal, non-contradictory is not non-being but true, complete, perfect being. The eternal, the absolute is primary; the temporal, historical, relative, is secondary.

The priority of the eternal over the historical is widely applied by Kierkegaard in his innumerable theological reasonings. He struggles with the "paradox" of the combination of the divinity and the historicity of Christ. Inasmuch as this topic does not present any interest for us, we limit ourselves to citing one typically Kierkegaardian statement on the matter: "What is historical is that God, the eternal, appeared at a given moment in time as an individual man." And as if apologizing for the god who lowered himself to historicity, he adds: "This is something not merely historical, but something historical of such a nature that could only be despite its essence...." (6, 16, II, 291)

It would seem that the "eternal" as a philosophical category is not reconcilable with any kind of dialectic. Nonetheless, Kierkegaard, with his characteristic scorn for logic and liking for paradoxes, stubbornly asserts a "dialectics of the eternal" (6, 16, II, 285) which is inaccessible to any kind of thought. "...The absolute," he says, "can be identified as absolute thanks to 'dialectics'." (6, 16, II, 285) Such a conception of "dialectics" is, obviously, closely akin to irrationalism.

But Kierkegaard has one category, playing a major role in his doctrine, which, for all his enmity towards "mediation," is intended as mediation of the temporal and the eternal. This category: "the moment," "the instant," "*öjeblikket*," "*momentum*," "*der Augenblick*," is "what everything revolves about." (6, 10, 48)

In *The Concept of Dread* Kierkegaard states the two-valued, double-unity nature of the category of "the moment," in which "time and eternity come into contact." (6, 11–12, 90) On the one hand, "history begins only with the instant," on the other, it is the authentic, eternal "now." In this connection Kierkegaard makes a critique of the "dialectics of the instant," as it is set forth in Plato's *Parmenides*, which Hegel called "the illustrious masterpiece of Platonic dialectics." (16, 10, 171) Kierkegaard rejects this doctrine as "dialectical witchcraft," (6, 11–12, 85) which identifies eternity with "the instant" as a temporal category whereas, to his mind, the instant is in essence "not an atom of time but an atom of eternity." (6, 11–12, 90) For all its transience, it is "full of eternity." (6, 10, 16)

The category of "the moment" plays a decisive role for Kierkegaard in his understanding of the passage to another quality, the abrupt arisal of the new. Interpretation of this passage as a moment determined by a free choice, by a decision, on the one hand avoids a rational-logical understanding of the leap as the passage of quantitative into qualitative change, and on the other hand links the temporary in man to the eternal, since the free choice realized in the moment is, Kierkegaard is sure, a Gift of God: "The moment is just that which does not ensue from the circumstances, it is something new, an intrusion of eternity.... The moment is a gift of heaven to the believer...." (6, 34, 327) These words are taken from the tenth and last number of Kierkegaard's paper *The Moment*, publication of which was prevented by Kierkegaard's death.

Kierkegaard's pathetic "dialectics" reaches its extreme of intensity in the analysis of "the moment." Spiritual calm, inertia, indifference are profoundly alien to Kierkegaard. His element is anxiety, agitation, fear and trembling, discontent. Precisely this reflection of anxious self-consciousness is just what he calls "existential dialectics" and what many adherents of Kierkegaard take for genuine dialectics, for a new, anti-Hegelian form of it worked out by Kierkegaard. But "existential dialectics" is just as alien to historical development, progress, the possibility of a conceptual, logical expression of the regularity of the origin and unity of opposites as it is to rest. The "existential dialectics" is not a dialogue; it is a monologue; it is reflective, introverted, introspective. By its very concept "existential dialectics" is not logical but alogical, paralogical. It is not even self-*knowledge*, psycho*logy*, since it does not tolerate generalizations, scientific abstraction, objectivity, conceptual fixation. What it counterposes to rest is not movement as development, as history, but anxiety, concentrated in the fleeting and decisive moment.

Hegel anticipated this form of consciousness, describing it in the *Phenomenology of Spirit*: "*This is unhappy consciousness, divided within itself*.... Here is the internal movement of *pure* mood, which *feels* itself, but feels agonizedly as the self-divided movement of infinite *melancholy*...." This thinking, in the words of the great dialectician, "remains the dissonant ringing of bells or warm wreaths of mist, musical thought that has not attained to the concept...." (16, 4, 112 and 116)

Even the very phrase "concept of dread" in the title of one of Kierkegaard's works, which J. Wahl calls "provocatory," has the ring of bitter irony on his own philosophy.

Some researchers give an evasive compromise answer to the question of Kierkegaard's relationship to the Hegelian dialectic. Wahl holds that "despite his opposition to the Hegelian dialectics, there is in Kierkegaard a recognition of dialectics, of existential dialectics, and a recognition of contradiction." (98, 29) In Gerdes' opinion, "it can not be denied that Kierkegaard took from Hegel his entire view of the transformation of the vital sense of all the existential expressions in dialectical movement," although he did remove its objective-logical content. (46, 24) R. Heiss asserts that "the great rivalry of Kierkegaard with Hegel is the rivalry of quarreling brothers." (55, 299) Actually, Kierkegaard's study of Hegel's dialectics accomplished nothing more than his ever-increasing alienation from it, extending to unconcealed hatred of the science of logic in general and dialectical logic in particular. The same Wahl distinctly formulated not what Kierkegaard learned in his antagonism to Hegel, but what he forgot: "And undoubtedly," he says, "the Kierkegaardian dialectics differs from the Hegelian dialectics, in that it does not recognize *Aufhebung*, inasmuch as it is sporadic, consists of leaps and breaches of continuity, inasmuch as it is lyrical and closely linked to subjectivity, finally because both its beginning and its end are not in itself but derive their motive power from a principle foreign to dialectics, namely God...." (96, 165) But in that case what is left of dialectics as logical self-development on the basis of the unity of opposites? And does this anti-dialectics have the right to appropriate the name of a method so opposed to it? Would not this be stretching the concept of "dialectics" to a point at which the opposition of incompatible philosophical principles and the mutually exclusive understanding of the laws and categories of dialectics disappear? But Kierkegaard totally excludes from his pseudo-dialectics any laws and conceptual logical categories. What is there in common between the dialectical method and a philosophy that condemns all method? Kierkegaard's "paradoxical irrationalism" is not a different species of dialectics; it is incompatible with dialectics in all its forms; it is a philosophy of a totally different genus.

In defiance of dialectics, whether objective or subjective, idealist or materialist, for Kierkegaard the fundamental laws of logic do not in principle allow the possibility of taking hold of or expressing movement, development, contradiction. And it is not a matter of elementary laws, of the laws of formal logic on the Aristotelian level, but of any possible logic, including the dialectical. For Kierkegaard, introducing contradiction, movement, transition into logic is a pretense, hypocrisy, dissimulation. All existence is irrational, so that as regards it all knowledge is powerless and all attempts to express it in any concepts whatsoever are inexorably doomed to fail.

Even in Kierkegaard's lifetime Alexander Hertzen wrote in his *Memoirs (Byloe i dumy)*: "I even believe that a man who has not *lived through* Hegel's *Phenomenology*...who has not *gone through* that fire and tempering, is not complete, is not modern." (20, 347) Kierkegaard lived through Hegelianism, went through that fire, but did not receive that temper; he tore himself out of the furnace and did everything in his power to extinguish the fire of the new, dialectical logic.

Post-Hegelian philosophy was at a crossroads. One of the roads that was open, the path of philosophical progress, was the path of removing the limitation of dialectical thought in a closed, completed, absolute system, by means of a radical transformation of the idealist dialectics into materialist dialectics. This road led through Feuerbach to Marx and Lenin. The other road, which idealist philosophy took, was a departure from the tradition begun by Descartes and completed by Hegel, the road through Kierkegaard to present-day existentialism.

In the first draft of the preface to the *Concept of Dread* the words in parentheses appeared: "My merit (as of Feuerbach as well) is my seriousness in the matter of the break (with Hegel – B.B.)" (6, 11–12, 272) But Feuerbach broke with Hegel's dialectics, dissociating himself from every kind of philosophical idealism, including the dialectical. Kierkegaard, on the other hand, rejected both the system and the method of

Hegel, dissociating himself from every kind of rationalism, including the idealist.*

Heiss is very wide of the mark when he declares that "comparison of Hegel with Marx, and also with Kierkegaard, thus shows that there is not *one* but many forms of dialectical understanding...." (55, 405) Now though comparison of Hegel with Marx does show that, comparison with Kierkegaard shows something else – that not everyone who calls himself a dialectician is one. It is one more verification that philosophers should not be judged by what they think of themselves; not, in any case by what Heiss, for example thinks of them: for him Kierkegaard is, along with Hegel and Marx, "one of the great dialecticians." (cf. 55)

Collins is right when he says that "although both of them subjected the Hegelian dialectic to sharp criticism, they moved far apart in their methods and results." (41, 49) They also differed completely in their motives. On this E. Rohde wrote: "Both of them spoke out against the dominant philosophy of their time, Hegelianism, but in a completely different way.... Marx wished to make Hegelian idealism (!) acceptable by...putting on its feet what Hegel had stood on its head; Kierkegaard's ambition was vastly more radical: he wanted to torpedo the entire Hegelian system from the ground up...." (89, 7) Rohde's total lack of comprehension of Marx' relationship to Hegel's idealism takes all the meaning out of the formula of Marx that he cites; Marx, of course, tried to make acceptable not Hegel's idealism but his dialectics, by liberating it from idealism. In this connection it is in order to adduce Collins' amusing remark in comparing the attitudes of Kierkegaard and Marx towards Hegel: "His [Kierkegaard's] proposed reform had nothing to do with the problem of putting the head and the feet where they belong, for the simple reason that a dialectical process has neither head nor feet, top nor bottom." (41, 49) And this very likely is not altogether unjust. But not by any means because, as Collins supposes, that Kierkegaard was on the other side of the fundamental question of philosophy, but because his doctrine does not stand either on its feet, as a metaphorical designation of objective reality, or on its head as a symbol of reason.

---

* In this respect Kierkegaard is closer to another prophet of irrationalism, his older contemporary Schopenhauer, who with his customary "profundity" called Hegel "a soulless, repulsive charlatan," and his dialectics "absolute balderdash." (*Parerga und Paralipomena*, Bd. I, Leipzig, s.d., p. 42–43)

CHAPTER IV

PATHETIC EGOCENTRISM

With all the resoluteness characteristic of him, Kierkegaard disputed Hegel's fundamental principle of the identity of being and thought, correctly regarding it as a reduction of being to thought. For him, being in general, and still more human existence, is not thought. Here Kierkegaard comes close to the Schellingian contraposition of possibility and actuality, limiting thought to the sphere of possibility and not extending it to actuality. For many writers on Kierkegaard this serves as grounds not only for denying the idealist nature of his philosophy but for presenting him as an implacable adversary of philosophical idealism. Thus, for example, Anz speaks of Kierkegaard as "a resolute critic of idealism." (29, 14) Johansen is of the opinion that although Kierkegaard does take as his starting point the spirituality of human nature, still his conception of spirit is such that it undermines the idealist conception. (63, 25–26) A correct answer to this question will define the place of Kierkegaard's doctrine both in the struggle of the two camps in philosophy and in the internecine strife of trends within the idealist camp.

Kierkegaard's polemic against Hegelianism is shot through with hostility to *objective* idealism, whose culminating expression is absolute idealism. Kierkegaard's opposition to objective idealism is intimately bound up with his intolerance of objective knowledge in general, which is closely tied to rationalism, especially panlogism. What repelled Kierkegaard from the *form* of idealism dominant in his day was not the denial of the primacy of the spiritual principle but the objective-logical approach to knowledge of it, the *science* of spirit.

For Kierkegaard any scientific understanding of the world is an evil, even if it is based on natural science. "The largest part of what flourishes at the present time most vigorously under the name of science (especially natural science) is not science at all but curiosity. In the last analysis, all sorts of disaster come from the natural sciences." (7, 241) Another entry in his diary runs: "If the natural sciences had been as developed in the time of Socrates as they are today, all the sophists would have been naturalists." (7, 246) In a word, science is not only useless but harmful curiosity, only repeating sophistical razzle-dazzle. But the most ruinous thing is when objective scientific knowledge invades the spiritual sphere.

"But all this sort of scientificity becomes most dangerous and injurious when it tries to penetrate into the sphere of spirit as well. Let them, if they must, concern themselves in their own way with plants, animals and minerals, but to treat the human spirit in that sort of manner, that is already blasphemy." (7, 243)

Man, in Kierkegaard's eyes, not only cannot be the object of scientific knowledge, he cannot even be regarded as subject-object, as conceived of by Feuerbach and various psychophysiological schools. He who exists cannot be in two places at the same time; he cannot be a subject-object." (6, 16, I, 190) "Materialist physiology is comical... but the newest, more sublimated physiology (referring to the doctrine of Carus – B.B.) is sophistical." (7, 243) The problem of body and spirit does not cause Kierkegaard any difficulties: spirit is primary, body secondary. "The body is the organ of the spirit and thereby is also spirit." (6, 11–12, 141) Kierkegaard's favorite formula: man is a synthesis of spirit and body, ruled by the spirit. In the last analysis, "man is spirit." (6, 24–25, 8) The idealist character of Kierkegaard's solution to the psychophysical problem is obvious.

But the psychophysical problem is only one of the aspects of the fundamental problem of philosophy, the question of the conception of being in its relation to thought. When Kierkegaard asserts, controverting Hegel, that being is not thought, that is in no way a renunciation of the idealist solution of the fundamental problem of philosophy but rather a renunciation of objective-idealist rationalism, since the essence of the divergence lies in the assertion or denial of *objective* reality, even when understood idealistically as the absolute idea, the logic of the world reason. The Hegelian identity of being and thought is rejected not because it asserts the secondariness of the material as other-being of the spiritual first principle but because in it spirit is identified with objectivity, with thought, with reason, with logic. For Kierkegaard being is not thought, just as spirit is not thought, which not only permits but demands logical measurement, a logical approach. This is the true meaning of his caustic remark that the statement that being and thought are one and the same is something at which "to laugh and weep at the same time." If the matter under discussion were not "being" but "existence" (in the specific meaning that Kierkegaard attaches to this term), not "thought" but "spirit" (again in the Kierkegaardian acceptation), then the principle of the identity of spirit and existence would adequately formulate existentialism as the Kierkegaardian form of *subjective* idealism.

What has been said is not at all controverted by Kierkegaard's polemic against the Cartesian "I think, therefore I am." Assuming that the inference from thinking to being is a contradiction (6, 16, II, 18), he advances against Descartes' formula the inverse relation between thinking and being: "Since I exist and am thinking, therefore I think." (6, 16, II, 33) Cartesianism dissects thinking and being, he adds; there is no "ideal identity" between them. Yet pure thought is very far from existence, Kierkegaard adds; more than that, "pure thought...has nothing, nothing in common with existence." (6, 16, II, 34) "Being that is identical with thinking is not at all human being." (6, 16, II, 3) The polemic is directed against "*pure* thought," "*ideal* identity," the reduction of spirituality to thought. The target of this polemic is not idealism but rationalism.

Kierkegaard's idealism differs not only from all objective idealism but also from subjective idealism of the Berkeleyan or even the Fichtean type; from contemplative or logicizing subjectivism, for which the subject is the first-given object, the first source of being and knowledge. Despite his constant references to the Socratic "know thyself," as the Ariadne's thread of philosophy, he brushes aside, from the outset, any kind of objective knowledge, even as self-knowledge. In no case, for him, does *self*-knowledge go over into *knowledge of the world*. Unlike Descartes or Fichte, he does not admit the idea of the passage from subjectivistic anthropology to ontology, to being as such, to the *non-Ego*, even to another *Ego*.

Objective reality is thrown overboard from Kierkegaard's philosophical craft, which pushed off from the *Ego* and sailed to God, who too is not an object but a subject. His entire philosophy, from start to finish, is not extroverted but introverted, directed not outside the self but inwards towards it. "Being" is expelled by "existence," meaning *my* human existence, self-knowledge, the internal world. Kierkegaardian "existence" is, as Jaspers says, "liberation from attachment to objects." (60, 253) Making the leap into "pure spirituality," (7, 273) Kierkegaard resolves the fundamental question of philosophy in the spirit of subjective idealism: "As Hamlet says, being and non-being have only a subjective meaning." (6, V, 141)

"My basic idea," Kierkegaard says, describing his entire literary activity, "was that in our time it has been forgotten, because of the abundance of knowledge, it has been forgotten what it means to exist and what significance *Innerlichkeit* has...." (6, 16, I, 242) The "knight of subjectivity" is absorbed in himself, sunk in himself, his sensations, moods, efforts. He is continually drawn "inward, into the abyss of the interior world." (6, 16, I, 26)

"Some naturalists," Kierkegaard wrote to Lund, "have found, or tried to find, a point of Archimedes existing somewhere in the world, and to observe the Universe from that point...." (6, 35, 4) He finds it within himself.

For him, "existence" in that specific sense is the only "actuality," limiting "being" and contraposed to "thinking." "Is the external world actuality?" he asks, and answers in the negative: "Actuality is the interior world *(Innerlichkeit)*, (6, 16, II, 26–27), the self-relation of ones *Ego* to one's *Ego*.

Although in Kierkegaard's view only that knowledge that is in an existential relation to existence is existential knowledge, self-knowledge is not, for him, a self-knowledge that objectivizes subjectivity. The interior world, which is not an object, cannot be the object of knowledge, and still less of scientific knowledge. It is impossible to think or speak of oneself in the third person. The *Ego* is inaccessible to expression, either by means of sense images or by means of concepts. It is immediate, and this immediacy is not contemplative but reflexive.

It is highly characteristic of Kierkegaard that he regards existence as "the only thing unknowable in itself, with which thinking has nothing whatever in common." (6, 16, II, 31) Inasmuch as for him existence is the only worthwhile object of philosophy, philosophy as a whole, as befits an irrationalism, does not care to have anything in common with thinking (despite the fact that it always does only that). Kierkegaard's works and diary are strewn with assertions of the alogical nature of existence, the impossibility of expressing it in concepts, in which it inevitably dissolves. In order to be related to existential actuality as such, it must be related not in thought but "paradoxically." But since existence is not something that *is* as a datum, but is continually becoming, it thereby, from the point of view of existential "dialectics", is inaccessible to logical understanding, to thinking reason.

After all that has been said, after the constant assertions that existence cannot be known, conceived, explained, but only lived, it comes as a surprise to hear Kierkegaard say: "I try with all my might to grasp my life with categories." (6, 4, 275) But is not categorial thinking the summit of conceptuality, which Kierkegaard regards as incompatible with existentialism? W. Anz, comparing Kierkegaard's doctrine with German classical philosophy, comes to the conclusion that "German idealism is the mass upon impact with which Kierkegaard got his categories," and "Kierkegaard's great achievement is that he worked out the category of existence, dissociating it from Hegel...." (29, 10 and 49) What is involved here is not the category of existence in the singular but a whole complex of categories of existence. Anz enumerates them: "existence," "paradox," "fear," "the moment," "passage," "the leap," "decision," "finitude"–"infinity," "possibility"–"actuality," "the Ego," "personality," "history," etc. (29, 10) E. Tielsch adds to the list: "reflexion," "suffering," "rebirth," "guilt," "sin." (cited from 67, VI, 154) But all of these are general concepts, which, of course, neither Kierkegaard nor any other philosopher can do without, but which cut at the root of his existentialist structure. When Sartre observes that "these categories are neither principles, nor categories, nor the content of concepts" (cited from 68, 54), he puts his finger on the internal contradictoriness of these "pseudo-concepts," these anti-conceptual concepts, these anti-categorial categories. It is no wonder that today's existentialists have preferred "existentials" to "categories" for marking the separation with the historical-philosophical tradition, even though that too does not free their irrationalistic *ersatz* concepts from the conceptuality they reject.

To their inventor, the "categories" of existence are a synonym of spiritual particularity, personal experiences. "Existence is always particular; the abstract does not exist." (6, 16, II, 33) When Kierkegaard speaks of subjectivity, he makes the reservation that he does not have the abstract concept of the subject in mind, "not pure humanity, pure subjectivity and the like..." (6, 16, II, 58), but the concrete, given subject for itself, *my* existence, the *Ego*. This fully justifies Hegel's description of the "unhappy consciousness," which, "endeavoring...to reach itself," "cannot grasp 'the other' as *particular* or as *actual*." (16, 4, 117)

Another important characteristic of "existence" is its emotional-voluntarist nature. The definition of man as a thinking being does not satisfy Kierkegaard; that is not the essence of man and that is not the thing that counts most in his existence. Descartes, Spinoza and Hegel were on the wrong road. "What is characteristically human is passion." (6, 4, 140) "Without passion it is impossible to exist." (6, 16, II, 12) "All the problems of existence are involved in passion." (6, 16, II, 55) In passion are the alpha and omega of existence. Passion first and foremost. It is both the motive force of existence and the "summit of subjectivity." The egocentric reflexion of existentialism is not self-contemplating but pathetic. "And this," says Kierkegaard, "is an aspect of the principle of subjectivity which so far as I know has never before been introduced or elaborated." (7, 434)

And so, according to the Danish theologian, man cannot be defined as a thinking substance, or as a unique existent, or in general as some kind of "object." Essentially, man cannot be defined at all; since he is a unique individuality, a purely subjective being, he makes himself what he is. For all Kierkegaard's seeming rejection of idealism, he does not leave the slightest doubt as to his adherence to subjective idealism. "Existence," in Kierkegaard's interpretation, is nothing other than the subjective-idealist answer to the fundamental question of philosophy. When Price cites Kierkegaard's formula: "Man is spirit. But what is spirit? The spirit is the self," and then asserts that Kierkegaard's view "should not be confused with subjectivism in the idealist sense...," (86, 37 and 119) he illicitly replaces adhesion to the idealistic camp in philosophy by the misleading limitation of idealism to certain particular forms of it – contemplative intuitionism and phenomenalism, from which it is true that the specific form of subjective idealism preached by the Danish theosophist does differ. For Kierkegaard, "existence," treated in a subjective-idealist manner, is not only the philosophical foundation of his idealism but also the springboard for his leap from idealism to religion. "That subjectivity, *Innerlichkeit*, is true and that existence is decisive on the road leading to Christianity...such was my idea." (6, 16, I, 278) By that admission Kierkegaard unmistakably defines the orientation of his existentialism. The bond between subjective idealism and religious fanaticism is his ethics, which gives Kierkegaard's answer to the question: "What does it mean to be a man?" (6, 16, II, 3), his reduction of the fundamental question of philosophy: "What does being mean?"

CHAPTER V

THE CRUCIFIXION OF REASON

For all their diversity of literary genres and mode of exposition, all Kierkegaard's works, whether lyrical outpourings or furious pamphlets, are in essence (if not in the text, then in their undercurrent) deeply religious, even in those cases in which they are directed against the church. His entire doctrine is a doctrine of faith and he has a right to call himself a "knight of the faith." "Strictly speaking," he writes, "the heart of all my literary activity is that I was essentially a religious man." (7, 316) By his own statement, his "literary work, taken as a *whole*, is religious from beginning to end." (6, 33, 5)

Kierkegaard regarded the ever-increasing atheism and lack of faith as the greatest evil on earth, disfiguring all human existence. "What is lacking in our times? Religiosity." (6, 16, II, 187) As Ibsen, who was under the influence of the Danish philosopher, said, "The wolf of cunning howls, barks at the sun of Christ's doctrine." (21, 3, 508) And all of Kierkegaard's work, all his life's activity, was an unceasing hunt of that wolf. Having reached the conclusion that the means formerly prevalent for defending and inculcating religious faith had broken down and were unavailing, he tried to forge new weapons, to establish new methods for dissipating unbelief, to find new means of healing the "fatal disease" "corrupting" the human soul. Christianity needs an offensive weapon, not a defensive one. (cf. 7, 290)

The philosophical foundation of Kierkegaard's dogma is his conception of "truth," his answer to Pontius Pilate's rhetorical question, "What is truth?" "Modern times," Kierkegaard says ironically of this, "modernized Christianity, has modernized Pilate's question," substituting for it the question: "What is madness?" (6, 16, I, 186)

Kierkegaard fiercely rejects the objectivity of truth and the criteria thereof. The scientific conception of truth is totally unacceptable to him either in its empirical or its rationalistic interpretation, either as correspondence with being or as correspondence with thought. Truth is not something objective, related to the object of knowledge. It is impossible to attain to the truth if it is approached objectively, as to some knowable object.

At the same time, Kierkegaard takes up arms against the dialectical conception of the historical relativity of truth which is characteristic of Hegel's philosophy. "According to Hegel truth is a consecutive world-historical process. Every society, every stage has its right and is only a moment of the true." (6, 16, I, 29) Distorting the Hegelian dialectic of the relative and the objective, Kierkegaard falsely attributes relativism to Hegel, identifying the historical process of learning with the sophism of Protagoras.

"For objectivity...is either an hypothesis or an approximation" (6, 16, I, 184), but by no means eternal truth, not truth with a capital letter. Kierkegaard contraposes to relative truth absolute truth as the only variety worthy of recognition and corresponding to the concept "truth." How far his "theory of knowledge" is from dialectics is visible even from the contempt with which he treats the historical process of knowledge, "the senseless speed with which one discovery cancels another. Who the devil can stand for that!" (6, 17, 138–139)

In counterbalance to the objective conception of truth and its criteria, Kierkegaard presents a subjective concept of truth. "I must find the truth which is the truth *for me*...." (8, 1, 31) Whereas objective truth leads away from the subject, the way to truth, as Kierkegaard sees it, is aimed at the subject. The subject decides what truth is, and this decision is the only criterion of truth. Kierkegaard concludes his argument by saying, "My thesis has been that subjectivity, *Innerlichkeit*, is truth." (6, 16, I, 296) Here conviction is not the result of objective observation, experimental investigation, logical proof, impartial authenticity. No, he writes, "The definition of truth is: objective uncertainty, retained in the mastering of a passionate internal effort, is truth, the highest truth attainable by the existent." (6, 16, I, 194) Asserting that the decision as to trueness "is based on subjectivity" (6, 16, I, 29), he breaks with the objective and hence with any rational solution of the question, erasing the distinction between *aletheia* (authenticity) and *doxa* (opinion) and converting "truth" into "belief," reducing objective authenticity to subjective belief. For him, correspondence to objective reality is inversely proportional to trueness. "The greater the objective authenticity, the less the *Innerlichkeit* (since *Innerlichkeit* [inward directedness] is precisely what subjectivity is); the less the objective authenticity, the greater the possibility of *Innerlichkeit*." (6, 16, I, 201)

But if the criterion of truth is subjective, if truth is the result of *my* will, *my* decision, free choice, is "the truth for me," it thereby loses its right to universality, general significance, singleness of meaning. The way is cleared for gnoseological pluralism, the recognition of multiplicity of truths, the way leading to gnoseological nihilism and the legitimation of mutually exclusive "truths." Kierkegaard's accusation of relativism, leveled against the Hegelian dialectic, turns against Kierkegaard himself. He does not draw these conclusions, which follow from his premises, since *his* "truth for me" is the only truth, Truth with a capital letter, incompatible with truths not for *him*, and rejecting them as not meeting the subjective criterion of truth, for which "subjectivity" is not a concept denoting every *Ego* but only *my Ego* as single and unique.

But does this not at once annul the opposition of the true and the false, truth and error? What is error, on this position? Kierkegaard himself raises the question. "In what does the criterion of the difference between truth and madness consist, if both are internally grounded in the same manner?" he asks. (6, 4, 269) But the question does not disturb Kierkegaard or shake his convictions as to the truth, his understanding of truth. "The statement that subjectivity is truth can not be made with greater internal confidence than when subjectivity primarily appears as untrue and none the less subjectivity is the truth." (6, 16, I, 205) "Thus," he concludes, "the individual is in possession of the truth even when he holds an untruth." (6, 16, I, 190) Here we have the consistent consequence of the subjectivistic conception of gnoseological arbitrariness.

This conception of truth serves as the basis for Kierkegaard's apology for religion. He insists, quite correctly, that theology, with its efforts down through the centuries to prove the truth of religion – empirically, historically, logically – has met with a fiasco, was bankrupted, went into decline. "Orthodox theology offers a depressing spectacle in our time...." (7, 290) And that is just because the orthodox want to base themselves on rational, speculative arguments and objective evidence, putting their reliance in speculative *theology*.

Kierkegaard sets as his goal discovering the reasons why theology does not live up to its vocation. The root of the evil is that orthodox theologians approach Christianity as a doctrine. "A false conception of Christianity always appears immediately when Christianity is converted into a doctrine and drawn into the sphere of intellectuality." (6, 16, II, 29) But "Christianity," says Kierkegaard, "is not a matter of knowledge" (6, 16, I, 206), it is indemonstrable by its very nature, it is not susceptible of proof. "...Objective knowledge of the truth of Christianity... is precisely what is untrue..." (6, 16, I, 215), since Christianity is inaccessible to objective knowledge. "Christianity protests against any kind of objectivity." (6, 16, I, 119)

Even posing the question of the necessity of proving, of justifying Christianity, is impermissible, according to Kierkegaard, since Christianity does not need proof and justification. How is it possible to prove that which is founded on faith? Faith does not allow of proofs; it regards them as its enemy. (cf. 6, 16, I, 26) If the truth is subjective, then all arguments as to the objective truth of Christianity are meaningless. In addition, it is impossible to demonstrate faith without its ceasing to be faith, based on subjectivity, born into life from within. "What is required," Kierkegaard declares, "is subjectivity; only in it is the truth of Christianity, if there is any at all; objectively there is none at all." (6, 16, I, 119) "For faith is not the result of straightforward scientific investigation.... On the contrary, with objectivity of that kind there is lost the infinite personal interest in passion, which is the condition of faith.... If passion is eliminated, nothing remains of faith either, since authenticity and passion can not be made into a team." (6, 16, I, 25)

Faith can not and should not count on the help of reason. Philosophy is unable to serve as a weapon of religion. The entire historical experience of theology bears witness to its feebleness, to the impossibility of a rational grounding of religious faith. "The intellect of a believer does not bring him any benefit." (6, 16, I, 217) The intellect is no friend of religion, but its adversary, the source of every doubt as to the truth of belief, the stimulus of unbelief. And these doubts can not be resolved on the basis of rational inferences. "What extraordinary metaphysical and logical efforts," Kierkegaard says, "have been exerted in our days to being a new, exhaustive, absolutely trustworthy proof of the immortality of the soul, combining all previous attempts; and the surprising thing is that at the same time confidence in immortality has decreased." (6, 11–12, 143) The intellect can not be the judge in matters of faith. It is a double-edged weapon that can not be depended on. Theology becomes a convenient target for the godless. That is where theology has brought religion! "How low Christianity has fallen, how wretched and helpless it has become! The intellect, that is what has emerged victorious...." (7, 420) Christianity must be rearmed for a new assault on the rising tide of unbelief.

It must be conceded, however, that there is a rational core in Kierkegaard's irrationalist conception: the assertion of the antagonism of religious faith and the trust, based in reason, of the irreconcilability of faith and knowledge, and the impossibility of rational proof of religious myths. But from this correct and well-grounded assertion Kierkegaard draws the conclusion: so much the worse for reason. It must be removed as an obstacle on the way to faith! It is typical that Kierkegaard, like all other irrationalists, for that matter, tries to prove irrationalism by using all his mental powers, every conceivable logical, rational inference and argument. To controvert rationalism, he directs its own weapons against it, relying on the very logic whose destruction is his purpose. Kierkegaard, in Sartre's words, "steals the language of knowledge in order to make use of it against knowledge." (cited after 68, 36)

He throws down the gauntlet to orthodox theology, which has turned into a philosophy which is the handmaid of dogma. But, for all his protestations, he does so with the aid of *his own* philosophical handmaiden, irrationalist philosophy. In the process philosophy, "the love of wisdom," turns into anti-philosophy.

Kierkegaard's repudiation of any proof of the existence of God is a concentrated expression of anti-theologism. "With what indefatigable zeal, with what an expenditure of time, with what assiduity and floods of words, have the speculative of our days endeavored to provide a solid proof of the existence of God! But to the same extent that the perfection of the proof increases, confidence in it decreases." (6, 11–12, 143) Kierkegaard returns again and again to this idea of the unrealizability, fruitlessness and needlessness of any proof whatsoever of this kind. The existence of God is not susceptible of any proof. In the last analysis, "proving the existence of anything that is before your eyes," he says, "is an outrageous insult, since it is an attempt to ridicule it." (6, 16, II, 256) Kierkegaard makes special criticism (as being typically speculative) of Anselm of Canterbury's ontological proof, which has been particularly successful with theologians. Following Kant's refutation of the ontological proof, Kierkegaard makes the reasonable assertion that in it being is replaced by the *concept* of being. Factual existence is independent of any definition of essence. The posing of the question of proving the existence of God is defective in itself: "If existence is not inherent in God, then it is impossible to prove his existence; but if existence is inherent in him, it is foolish to try to prove it." For as soon as I begin the proof, I thereby not only bring his existence into doubt but start from the assumption of his non-existence. (6, 10, 36)

Moreover, God is not one of the objects whose existence can be the subject of objective knowledge. God is a subject and as such is accessible only to a subjective approach. In addition, Kierkegaard remarks shrewdly, "God cannot prove his existence in any other way than by swearing to it; but for him there is nothing higher that he could swear by." (5, 2, A394)

Kierkegaard counterposes faith in God to any kind of proof whatsoever. His existence cannot be proved; it must be believed in. "...Faith is not knowledge but an act of freedom, an expression of will." (6, 10, 80) What has to be done is to have faith, and not to gain conviction by logical inferences. Whatever understanding of the question there may be, where there is no faith there is neither God nor his existence. God *is* only for him who believes in him devotedly, unquestioningly, recklessly. The existence of God is established not by proof but by submission, by worship. Unbelief is not the result of lack of understanding but the consequence of insubordination, rebelliousness, disobedience. And the battle against it must be waged not by rational inferences but by edification and pacification. "...The existence of God is asserted not by proofs but by adoration." (6, 16, II, 256) Not objectivity but the subjectivity of faith in God, coming from within, is the only way to him. Such a subjectivity does not exclude transcendence, but rather requires and asserts it. Divine transcendence is "the consequence of the principle of subjectivity." (7, 2, 123) For Kierkegaard, the emotional-voluntarist principle, and not the rational principle, is the primary source and the guarantee of religious faith.

Kierkegaard was led to his scorn for traditional theology by his deep disappointment in it. The basis of this disillusionment was the indisputable truth that it is impossible to give a rational justification for religion, that there is an irreconcilable antagonism between faith and knowledge. Faith did not demand confidence in reason, but rather that it be discredited, belittled, humbled. In line with Kierkegaard's favorite formula, it was necessary to make a choice: either–or. And he unhesitatingly puts reason aside as a hindrance, an obstacle on the way to whole-hearted, fanatical faith. The necessity of asserting religion at all costs led him to a militant irrationalism. "I have tried just now to show why Christianity and philosophy do not admit of being combined," is the basic principle of his anti-philosophy. (7, 1, 52) Kierkegaard set as his aim "the utmost irrationalization of Christianity." (96, 133) Christianity has no part whatsoever in the realm of rational knowledge. Faith has nothing in common with knowledge. The intrusion of the intellect into the spiritual scene is unwarranted and impermissible. There it is powerless. "While reason, like a despairing passenger, stretches his hand vainly out towards the shore, faith, with all its inherent energy, acts in the depth of the soul, and joyfully and victoriously saves the soul in spite of reason." (6, 16, I, 216) The intrusion of reason into the concerns of faith is not only useless but harmful: for eating the fruit of the tree of knowledge was the original sin that from Adam's time down to the present weighs on all of humanity. Kierkegaard speaks flatly of "the sin of reason." (cf. 7, 551)

Kierkegaard's effort to come to grips with the intellectual approach puts him in sharp conflict with the philosophy of the Enlightenment, to the "enlightening or artificial foolishness," as he calls it his *Diary*. (7, 638) And in opposition not only to the philosophy of the Enlightenment but to enlightenment as such, for "the more culture and knowledge, the more difficult it is to become a Christian." (6, 16, II, 88) With bitter irony he deplores the growth of rationality: "If statistical tables were drawn up for the growth of demand for intellect from generation to generation, as tables are drawn up for the demand for alcohol, we should be astonished at the way that demand has grown in our time...." (6, 17, 72)

The objective way of thinking of the natural sciences, which grows into the scientific world view, is disastrous for religion. "That is just the seat of the delusion, when it is asserted that science leads to God." (7, 242) It only interferes with understanding of the Scriptures. God is not to be found in knowledge of nature. "...All this scientific gang," as Kierkegaard calls natural science, "is especially dangerous and demoralizing when the attempt is made to transfer it into the territory of spirit," replacing religion by science. (cited after 58, 284) Let science know its place; let it not go beyond its prescribed limits of the objective knowledge of things; let it not intrude on the spiritual sphere, which is foreign to it. It proposes to know everything under the sun, whereas "the highest degree of understanding conceivable would be understanding of what cannot be understood." (6, 16, I, 205)

"I shall show," asserted Immanuel Kant, "that reason cannot achieve anything either in one way (the empirical) or in the other (transcendental) and that it spreads its wings in vain when it tries, by means of mere speculation, to go beyond the limits of the sensibly perceptible world." (22, 3, 516) Criticizing "any theology based on the speculative principles of reason" (22, 3, 544), Kant regarded it as necessary to restrict reason in order to leave room for faith. Kierkegaard, taking this as his starting point, directed his criticism in an entirely different direction; in contrast to Kant, he did not admit of religion within the limits of reason alone, and the Christian faith as "*scientific* faith," (23, 172), regardless of the fact that Kant is referring not to the theoretical but to the practical reason which, he says, convinces us that "morality inevitably leads us to religion." (23, 6) This last assertion too, as we shall see, is denied by Kierkegaard, in whose opinion, on the contrary, religion leads to morality (or rather what he calls morality).

Still less sufferable to him is the Hegelian philosophy of religion, which is one of the fundamental motives for his irreconcilable hostility towards Hegelianism. "For me," Kierkegaard writes, "it is simply impossible to avoid laughter when I think of the Hegelian conception of Christianity." (7, 448) Another entry in his diary runs: "...Basically, Hegel makes man a heathen possessing a reason like that of the animals." (7, 446) At the same time Hegel would have us believe that "it is precisely his philosophy that is the highest development of Christianity." (6, 36, 109)

In Kierkegaard's decisive condemnation of Hegel's philosophy of religion, as in all his philosophy, there is nothing surprising. The two men chose diametrically opposite methods of apologetics for Christianity and defending it from the Enlightenment. While Kierkegaard divorces faith from reason and religion from philosophy, for Hegel philosophy is the only solid bulwark of religion, reason is the fortress of faith. "Reason," in Hegel's words, "is the only soil on which religion can be at home." (52, 126)

In his *Lectures on the Philosophy of Religion* Hegel aimed at "directly and openly developing religion from reason." (52, 20) In so doing he believed that the philosophy of the Enlightenment, which tended towards atheism, had to be opposed by rational knowledge of God, which he saw as the essential need of his epoch. "The proposition that God rules the world as *Reason* would be *irrational* unless we recognized that the expression relates equally to religion...." (52, 25) Accordingly, "reason has a right to show what kind of religious doctrine is its theme." (52, 26) And as if anticipating Kierkegaard's religious position, Hegel attacks the assertion that "the knowledge of God should not be based on the concepts of reason but that awareness of God flows only from feeling." No, he objects, "God is not the product of weakness, hope, fear, joy, etc.; what is based only on my feeling exists only for me.... God is not rooted in feeling alone, is not only *my* God.... Thus, the philosophy of religion is faced with the demand to prove God." (52, 27) "Feeling is only subjective, appertaining to me as a given individual." (52, 30) One could imagine that Hegel said this after reading Kierkegaard, but it is a transcript of lectures delivered for the last time in the year of Hegel's death, when the eighteen-year old Kierkegaard was just beginning his studies, or rather scorning them.

No, Kierkegaard protested when reading Hegel later, faith and reason are "heterogeneous"; faith must sever from itself reason, which is alien to it. It is senseless to seek faith in philosophy. It is impossible to overcome the Enlightenment with the arms of logic; to do battle with it, all rationalism must be eradicated from human consciousness. "*Back* from system, from the speculative, etc. to become a Christian," Kierkegaard appeals. (6, 33, 50)

It is not only that "if we could establish a system of being, we should thereby have explained life, and faith would be superfluous" (59, 50), but also that at every step of his life the believer comes up against the barbed wire of reason entangling his belief. This is why Kierkegaard was convinced, not without reason, of the destructive effects for religion of being invaded by reason corroding it from within. A rationalized Christianity entails the speculative deformation of all religious dogmas. In the words of Tübingen theologian Anz, Hegel reasons like a thinker and "not like a believer; he is not founded on faith...but interprets religious ideas, understood in an idealist sense, in their ontological structure." (29, 51)

But religion understood in such a manner is not genuine religion, the religion of revelation, but a secularized, laicized pseudo-religion.

E. Geismar, a prominent Danish student of Kierkegaard, formulates Kierkegaard's relation to Hegel very accurately by saying that for Kierkegaard Hegel is the worst enemy of Christianity, since "while seeming to defend Christianity with all the tools of thought, he actually betrays it...." (45, 251) "...The Hegelian philosophy...is at a crossroads: it must either break unconditionally with Christianity or relinquish the designation of a 'Christian philosophy.' But the Hegelian philosophy does neither the one nor the other...." (6, 33, 137) Extremes meet: Kierkegaard's judgment as to the relationship of Hegelianism to Christianity has much in common with the views of the Left Hegelians, who were convinced that atheism lurks within Hegel's doctrine. It is no accident that such a militant atheist as Feuerbach was convinced of this even before he broke with idealism. And if the statement of Schrempf, the translator, commentator and adherent of Kierkegaard: "Hegel leads directly to Feuerbach" (cited after 96, 128) and still more Anz's statement: "Kierkegaard's critique of Hegel was justified. Hegel was not a Christian philosopher," (29, 55), are one-sided exaggerations, they still contain an element of potential truth. It must not be forgotten that for Hegel religion is a lower, transitional stage of the development of spirit, as compared with philosophy, that the concepts of philosophy "subsume" into a higher synthesis the forms of art and the ideas of religion. For him, *believing* on a pre-philosophical and anti-philosophical plane "means nothing other than not being able to advance to a determinate idea, not being willing to enter into further consideration of the content. That particular people and strata, not in possession of intellectual culture, should be satisfied with indeterminate ideas is fully understandable. But if the developed mind, and interest in the thoughtful consideration of what is recognized as being of higher, and even the highest interest, are prepared to be satisfied with indeterminate ideas, then it becomes hard to decide whether in point of fact the spirit relates *seriously* to that content." (16, 3, 363)

For all of Hegel's enormous superiority in "culture of the intellect," in the question at issue, the harmony or disharmony ("heterogeneity") of faith and reason, of religion and science, it is Kierkegaard who is right here, not Hegel. A rational, intellectual religion is a *contradictio in adjecto*, self-deception on the part of the philosopher. What conclusion should be drawn from this is another matter. But the choice, "either–or," is absolutely unavoidable.

Sören Kierkegaard is perhaps the most brilliant representative of fideism in the European philosophy of the first half of the nineteenth century. His entire philosophy is an apologia for fideism, and not merely a defense of it but an aggressive attack on anti-fideism.

For Kierkegaard, as has already been observed, faith requires of man the renunciation of reason. It "begins precisely at the point where reason leaves off." (6, 4, 56) Reason must make way for faith. For faith is either a *pre*-judgment ("The best proof of the immortality of the soul or of the existence of God, etc., is, strictly speaking, the corresponding impression thereof obtained in childhood, or in other words, this proof, in contrast to the numerous learned and eloquent proofs, may be formulated as follows: this is thoroughly trustworthy, because that is what my father told me" [7, 313–314]) or faith is a *super*-judgment *(Ueberzeugung)* which is superior to any and all proofs. (cf. 7, 251) On Kierkegaard's philosophical banner is inscribed: "Thou shalt believe" (7, 451), unconditionally, unthinkingly, at all costs.

What we have here is not the "Danish Socrates" but the Danish Tertullian. E. Brunner is right when he says that "if anyone at any time used the catchword *credo quia absurdum*, it was Kierkegaard." (40, 310) "Hardly any other church father," Kierkegaard wrote in his *Diary*, "stood for Christianity in the interest of God as strongly as Tertullian." (7, 516) This is said of the relentless persecutor of philosophizing heretics, the man who cried in the *De prescriptione hereticorum* (Sec. 7): "Wretched Aristotle!... Down with every attempt to concoct an ill-assorted Christianity diluted with Stoicism, Platonism and dialectics! After Jesus Christ we need no curious disputes, after the Holy Gospel no investigations." And Kierkegaard was just as indignant at the "heresy" of the Hegelianizing theologians.

Can there be any doubt that Kierkegaard's notions of faith and reason are nothing but fathomless fideism? Can there be any doubt as to the fideism of a philosopher who said: "The task is not to understand Christianity but to understand that it is impossible to understand it.... That is the sacred affair of faith...." (7, 326) And yet there is no lack of religious philosophers who not only doubt it but are even ready to deny it. Thus, for example, neo-Thomist Collins asserts that Kierkegaard's point of view "is not an antilogical and irrational standpoint, but rather one which would insist upon the difference between logic and metaphysics...logic prescinds from, and is indifferent to, real existence." (41, 121) Merely that! But neo-Thomist philosopher Jolivet (as we know, the Catholic Church formally condemned fideism, although in essence Catholic theology too, setting faith above knowledge, is fideistic) flatly recognizes the "deeply fideistic" character of Kierkegaard's thought, Lutheran in its sense (64, 101). And the militant Catholic Garelik, strongly condemning Kierkegaard's Protestant fideism, even entitled his book "Kierkegaard's Anti-Christianity." On the other hand, Collins, a more complaisant neo-Thomist poses the question: "Is this an instance of fideism?" and answers: "It seems likely that the answer must be in the negative." (41, 147) As for Protestant theologians, we shall see that as a rule they try, in defiance of logic, to prove the undemonstrable, the possibility of reconciling Kierkegaard's fideism with rational knowledge.

For Kierkegaard faith is something purely subjective, proceeding from within an emotional-voluntaristic attitude to "truth." "Faith is the highest passion of subjectivity." (6, 16, I, 121) The believing man is not the thinking man. The Cartesian *cogito, ergo sum* is displaced by the *credo, ergo sum*. In this conception truth is identical with belief. And despite Kierkegaard's protestations, this conception differs radically from that of Socrates. Objective comprehension of God, he is convinced, would only attest unbelief in him, since God is to be believed in just because it is impossible to know him. Faith, extreme subjectivity, becomes "absolute objectivity." And nonetheless Kierkegaard controverts his own view by his actions: he controverts what he proves by what he proves. His method is a graphic illustration of the self-refutation of irrationalism. "Here, apparently, is a basic and even fatal discrepancy between (1) Kierkegaard's conclusion that, since faith is higher than reason, it does not admit of nor require rational grounds, and (2) the fact that two of his principal philosophical works, especially the *Concluding Unscientific Postscript*, are a rational underpinning of faith." (47, 93; retrans. from the Russian)

The basic category, the core of Kierkegaard's entire philosophy, is "faith." In him the fundamental question of philosophy takes the form of what the relationship is between "the truth of faith" and the objective truth of knowledge. The subjective-idealist conception of "truth" enables him not only to extend the concept of "truth" to subjectively motivated religious faith but also to dissolve "truth" in "faith," the axis around which his entire world view revolves. "It is clear," an entry in his *Diary* runs, "that in my works I have given a broader definition of faith than there has ever been previously." (7, 488) Even some present-day bourgeois philosophers hold "that Kierkegaard's philosophical originality consists in his conception of faith." (68, 286) The point of departure of his definition of that concept is the contraposition of faith to knowledge, the approach to faith as anti-knowledge. It may be said, therefore, that gnoseology, epistemology, the theory of knowledge, turns in Kierkegaard into fideology, pisteology (Greek *pistis*, faith), into the theory of belief.

In Kierkegaard's words, "*faith*, defined specifically, is different from every other kind of acquisition and immanence *(Innerlichkeit)*," for passion, which is characteristic of faith, and reflexion, which is characteristic of knowledge, including self-knowledge, "are mutually exclusive." (6, 16, II, 325) Faith is an act of the will, of free choice, of passionate inclination.

The *will* to faith is of decisive importance for Kierkegaard, and conditions *decision* by free *choice*. "Faith is not an inference but a decision, precluding any doubt." (6, 10, 81) And every decision is rooted in the subject, depends entirely on himself. And for Kierkegaard the decision of the subject when faced with such a choice is *pre*-decided, he cannot but choose faith. He *must* make, cannot but make "a choice whose truth is: here there can be no question of choice." (7, 447)

Such a decision is a "qualitative leap," a "moment," passage into a different spiritual state, whose distinctive feature is devotion. "...Hic Rhodus, hic salta," Kierkegaard exclaims. (7, 248) At this instant "man becomes a new vessel and a new creature."

A decision calls for decisiveness. It entails risk. "Without risk there is no faith; the greater the risk, the greater the faith." (6, 16, I, 201) Reading these passionate, inspired fideistic outpourings of Kierkegaard, one recalls Hertzen's words about the self-expression of feelings and impulses, absorbing the individual: where there is no understanding, "there can be frankness but there cannot be *truth*." (19, 5) The Danish God-seeker might say: "Illusion that exalts us is dearer to me than the abyss of lower truths," fanatical religious self-deception.

But there is a deep cleft in Kierkegaard's subjectivist fideism, which the "knight of subjectivity" tries vainly to bridge: the cleft between the voluntarist self-determination of the believer and divine revelation. But of course there is nothing improbable for the believer. He can attain to the unattainable, have access to the inaccessible. "Faith itself is a miracle...." (6, 10, 62)

Here is still another basic difference between Kierkegaardianism and Socratism, which Kierkegaard himself remarks. The truth of faith is obtained directly "from the hand of God," and the true teacher and mentor of man is none other than God himself. (6, 10, 13) Therefore, the primary source of faith is divine revelation and not subjective impulse in and of itself. "...In the Christian conception, truth does not reside in the subject, however, but in revelation, which had to be announced." (7, 325) Accordingly, behind the immanence of faith lies the transcendental genesis of truth.... Fideism is not unbounded, but laps at dogmatic shores.

For all its alienation from reason, fideistic idealism is not mere folly. It grasps and absolutizes, hyperbolizes the psychology of religious faith and religious feeling and gives it an emotional description, a kind of phenomenology of religious intentionality, delimiting and contrasting faith and reason, sacrament and knowledge. But description, no matter how vivid and expressive it may be, is not by any means an understanding or explanation of the phenomenon described. Understanding of the psychological process that gives rise to and reinforces the religious feeling was something Kierkegaard could not achieve, and his explanation was false and spurious. The social and socio-psychological determinants of religious faith were *terra incognita* to Kierkegaard.

If "faith" is the central category of Kierkegaard's fideology, "paradox" is the categorial key to his understanding of "faith." "The distinguishing mark of Christianity is paradox, absolute paradox" (6, 16, II, 250), and Kierkegaard very zealously tries to convince the reader of the necessity of paradox. In the last analysis, "the truth *is* a paradox," the highest truth. "The highest thing to which human thought can strive is to go beyond its own limits, reaching paradox." (6, 16, I, 97) Paradox, which is objective inaccuracy, is at the same time truth (6, 16, I, 196) "since the only thing that can be understood about it is that it cannot be understood" (6, 16, I, 209); if paradox were intelligible, it would no longer be paradox. And the most paradoxical thing for thought is its paradoxical relation to paradox: it wants nothing so much as to comprehend what it is impossible to think. The unthinkable, paradox, is an unquenchable passion for thought and, like every passion, is suffering for thought. "When paradox and judgment conflict in their mutual understanding of their difference, their interrelation is happy, like understanding in love, in attraction, to which we have not yet given a name and give it only afterwards." (6, 10, 46)

Like every passion, paradox is linked to risk. But the risk is great, since paradox as truth is *absurd*. Yes, absurd. Kierkegaard takes up the challenge that Tertullian has flung to reason. He does not flinch at calling things by their names: a paradox that is realized, invited, assimilated, is nothing other than absurd. Faith holds fast to it, and it calls for disdain of reason, "the enslavement of reason." "The absurd is precisely the object of faith and the only thing in which it is possible to have faith," and "it is just because of the rejection of the objective that the absurd is the strength, the standard of faith...." (6, 16, I, 202) In order to perform the act of faith, Kierkegaard says, I must "close my eyes and immerse myself, with full confidence, in the absurd." (6, 4, 31) And by immersing myself in it, by having faith, I convince myself that my faith is not absurd, not at all, it remains absurd only for him who has no faith. Here is, in all its clarity and ugliness, the "qualitative leap," Kierkegaard's dialectics.

But if the object of faith is absurdity, then for the believer there is nothing simpler and more natural than miracles: "What is surprising about the fact that paradox is surprising?" (6, 10, 50); "a miracle is a miracle and cannot be understood." (6, 4, 73)

Kierkegaard has not said anything new on this "question" as compared with what had been said by Tertullian 1700 years before him. "The Son of God was born, as is every child; and there is not shame in that, although the fact itself is shameful. The Son of God died, as does every man; and that fact is fully probable, although it is an absurdity. And he rose from the dead; the fact is certain just because it is impossible." (*De carne Christi*, Sec. 5) Following in Tertullian's footsteps, Kierkegaard often returns to the absurdity of the god-man, the coming into being in time of the eternal god, the growth of Jesus from childhood to maturity, the incarnation of the Holy Ghost, his death and resurrection. The miraculous is unintelligible and undemonstrable. It is a miracle precisely because it is inaccessible to reason and incomprehensible by it. Only Hegelians do not admit of any miracles. (6, 16, I, 174) In the *School of Christianity* we find a typically Tertullian-like tirade: "Fortunate is he who is not dismayed, but believes that Jesus Christ fed five thousand people with five loaves of bread and two fishes...who believes that Jesus Christ said to the man sick with the palsy: 'Thy sins are forgiven thee... arise, take up thy bed, and go....' " (6, 26, 71) It is not only useless, but impermissible to make an historical investigation as to whether Jesus existed, or to attempt to prove his historical reality, as Strauss and Bauer did. "We cannot 'know' anything about Christ since, being a paradox, an object of faith, he exists only for the believer. Any historical narrative is only a statement of knowledge...." (6, 26, 23)

Such is Kierkegaard's fideism, the cornerstone of all his doctrine and all of his philosophy in general – the *reductio ad absurdum* of philosophy, a proof of his own teachings by reducing them to the absurd. The proof of the unprovability of faith does not lead Kierkegaard to unbelief; on the contrary, it leads him irresistibly to unreason, to unthinking faith.

Contrasting Kierkegaard's doctrine with Hegel's panlogism, Allison has well given it the name of "misologism," hatred of logic. If we follow the judgments of reason, then, according to Kierkegaard, religion will inevitably appear to us in the form of illusion. And no kind of higher reason, going beyond ordinary judgment, will help, since higher reason is still only reason. The only fitting function of reason is negative. The believer "employs reason only to the extent that by means of it he takes note of the unknowable, to which he relates with faith, against reason." (6, 16, II, 280) The works of Kierkegaard are a clear illustration of how sometimes human reason applies all its powers and possibilities, all its ingenuity and inventiveness to convince itself and others of its powerlessness, of its own inability to convince.

It is amusing to see the discussion among Kierkegaard scholars as to whether the fideism of the Danish philosopher was against reason or only above reason. As we know, the latter formulation is the traditional means of masking fideism in this one of its forms, which does not totally reject reason but sets theological limits to its application. Of course, reason within the limits of faith, with a constant looking back at the dogmas of the church, is a mutilated reason in bondage to fideism. But Kierkegaard's "unbounded" fideism denies philosophy altogether. Such a fideism is not at all to the taste of Catholic neo-Thomism, nor to that of those Protestant theologians who are concerned about the modernization of Lutheranism towards meeting the questions of today's educated man.

But no matter how hard the Kierkegaardians strive to convince their readers that the theme of their inspirer is aimed at a faith that is not against reason but above it, a faith that comes into operation only at heights unattainable by finite human reason, unequivocal statements by Kierkegaard himself definitely refute their fideistic opportunism. Allison is right in saying that "despite the protestations of many modern commentators, this position should be regarded as radically irrationalistic." (Cited from 47, 135; retrans. from the Russian)

The neo-Thomists, who present their fideism in a philosophical wrapping, dissociate themselves from the frank open fideism of Kierkegaard and distinguish the super-rational from the anti-rational, although the two actually are only two versions of fideism. This enables them, in contradistinction to Protestant irrationalists, to present Kierkegaard's fideism as it really is. "Faith, according to Kierkegaard," Jolivet writes in this connection, "is against reason, and not merely above it. It is the death of reason." (65, 80) It is in this that Collins sees the difference of Kierkegaard from the Catholic irrationalism of Pascal.

Kierkegaard can be accused of all sorts of things but not of a lack of frankness and straightforwardness in defending a fideism imbued with the urge "to believe despite reason." (6, 16, II, 278) Man must "discover that there is something that directly contradicts his thinking and his reason." (6, 16, II, 377–378) He calls for "nailing reason to the cross of faith." (6, 16, II, 276) And H. Garelick may well be right when in answer to the question: "Above or against reason?" he says: "Both." (44)

Kierkegaard's doctrine as to the sources and essence of religious faith leads us inevitably to thinking of Feuerbach. It is a kind of Feuerbachianism with a minus sign. In it are clearly shown the characteristic traits of religion, perceived and thought through in the positive sense in the *Essence of Christianity*.

Kierkegaard was acquainted with the works of his older contemporary, the great German atheist, and more than once refers to people who "want to be Feuerbach and imperiously dismiss all religion." (6, 36, 6) For Kierkegaard, Feuerbach is the "insidious demon" who got at the secret of religion, and for that reason he "saw in Feuerbach at once an unwitting ally and an open opponent" (39, 36), an enemy with whose opinion he had to reckon: "*Ab hoste consilium.*" (8, 3, 249) Kierkegaard saw the demoniacal insight of Feuerbach's critique of religion in Feuerbach's realization that the secret of theology is anthropology, and cites, approvingly, the corresponding formula from the *Essence of Christianity*. Their *concordia discors* (dissonant harmony) consists in the fact that both, from the right or from the left, opposed Hegel's treatment of religion and both held that the liquidation of theology is the logical consequence of the Hegelian postulates. Kierkegaard refers to Feuerbach, pointing out that even such an irreconcilable opponent of religion sees its roots in subjectivity, feeling, passion, suffering. Kierkegaard's attitude towards the views of his diametrical opposite is convincing testimony of the acuteness of Feuerbach's critique of religion and the depth of his analysis of the psychology of faith.

Kierkegaard's commentators frequently declare that for all his hostility to Hegel's philosophy, the Danish detractor made wide use of the dialectical method, while Feuerbach, in breaking with idealism, at the same time rejected the dialectical mode of thinking. Acquaintance with Kierkegaard's fideistic conception gives a very clear understanding of what his widely self-acclaimed existential, "double," "pathetic" dialectics, or "superdialectics" really represents.

The dialectic method that Hegel elaborated in every direction was directed, for all its limitations as a system of absolute idealism, against the limitation of the understanding; it is super-discursive. Even in the very term of *Verstand* in German we can hear ver*stehen* – limitation, staticity, immobility of thought, and Hegel contraposes to this immobility reason *(Vernunft)*, which opens up unlimited perspectives to dialectical logic. Putting aside metaphysics does not lead us out of the sphere of logic, but enlarges its orbit. Kierkegaard's line leads in exactly the opposite direction. It not only imprisons logical thought but also represses reason; what it opposes to formal-logical judgment is not dialectical reason but absurdity, paradox, "scandalous" faith. Hegel leads logical thought to dialectics; Kierkegaard's "paradoxical dialectics" leads away from logical thinking. "In speaking of what absolute paradox, absurdity, the unknowable can, should and wants to be, we come upon the passionate desire to establish dialectically the distinguishing feature of unknowability." (6, 16, II, 273) What is meant is "dialectically hidden religious passion." (6, 16, II, 215) Kierkegaard rejects the "pretension" of science to dialectics (6, 16, II, 267), which actually, he says, does not appertain to science but to religion; religion is dialectical in all its forms and paradoxically dialectical in Christianity. (ibid.) Contradiction as paradox, paradoxical treatment of the "qualitative leap," recognition of the "dialectics" of the eternal, unchanging, inaccessible, the absolute alternative as counterpoise to the unity of opposites as the basic law of dialectics – all this is worlds removed from dialectical logic and in essence has nothing in common with it. In his *Zerstörung der Vernunft* the Hungarian philosopher György Lukács convincingly exposes the real historico-philosophical role of Kierkegaard's "dialectics" as an alogical reaction to dialectical logic, as an irrationalist distortion of dialectics. (cf. 78, 78)

Kierkegaard's pseudo-dialectics is just as much a handmaid of religion as scholasticism was. It is his "new militant theological doctrine." (9, 2, 192) The old monastic wine is poured into new bottles. "In its truth," Kierkegaard says of his "dialectics," "it is a voluntary auxiliary force, helping to discover and find where the absolute object of faith is located...precisely at the point where knowledge comes up against its difference from lack of knowledge and bows down in absolute veneration before ignorance...." (6, 16, II, 199)

"Paradoxical dialectics" is nothing but the degeneration of dialectics into mysticism; it is a "dialectics of faith," (cf. 6, 4, 34) "paradoxical mysticism." (cf. 34, 86) It "asserts its idealism as an historical form of the mystical." (27, 219) Some interpreters deny this. Price, for example, answers "No" to the question: "Was Kierkegaard a mystic?" (86, 188), on the grounds that the mystic denies that God is unattainable, and that the personality of the mystic is absorbed into the divine, whereas Kierkegaard is egocentric, and for him God remains unattainable to the believer. But in so doing, Price unwarrantedly narrows the concept of mysticism, failing to see the variations in it. To be sure, Kierkegaard's paradoxical mysticism differs from the abstract-contemplative mysticism of, for example, Jakob Böhme. Jolivet is closer to the truth on this matter; he says "that if the term 'mysticism' is taken in a broader sense...there is nothing to prevent us and rather everything to induce us to speak of Kierkegaard's mysticism.... In Kierkegaard mysticism passes from he cognitive plane to the plane of will." (64, 210–211) But does that not mean that the will to faith cloaks the "cognitive plane" as well in an impenetrable mystical cloud?

Kierkegaard's paradoxical mysticism did not escape the fate of every irrationalism – self-refutation. Applying all his uncommon mental abilities to proving logically the insolvency of logical thinking, he casts doubt on the probative force of his alogism. "His philosophy terminates in a rejection of those very principles of logic on which he proceeded as a philosopher," of all his "therefore," "if–then," etc. (36, 15) For "any attempt to deny reason must employ reason and the laws of logic." (44, 17) Calling for the crucifixion of reason, Kierkegaard is not able to do without it. Reason's attempt at suicide cannot be carried out.

CHAPTER VI

NARCOTIC ETHICS

The fundamental category of Kierkegaard's entire philosophy, "existence," discloses all its ethical content upon closer examination. "Only ethical and ethical-religious knowledge are essentially related to existence and being." (6, 16, I, 188) Kierkegaard speaks explicitly of his existentialism as an "ethical world view." (6, 16, I, 114) "Existence" has a vector, directional, striving character. "The ethical is and remains the highest task set every human being." (6, 16, I, 141) There are no more important, more significant, questions than that of how to live, what to be, towards what to strive. "Existence" is nothing other than the search for an answer to this question, a *choice* of the answer and the carrying out of it, carrying it over into life, the formation of life in correspondence with that choice. "To reinforce for myself what is cardinally necessary to me, *what I should do*! The question for me is not what I should know... for me it is rather the question of understanding my vocation...." (7, 43)

The identification of "existence" with "actuality" appears in all its introvertedness in this connection. "...The proper ethical actuality of the individual is the only actuality...." (6, 16, II, 287) That activity cannot be the object of objective knowledge, but only the content of the individual's self-consciousness. "...Ethically, the individual is infinitely interested solely and exclusively in his own actuality." (6, 16, II, 25) Ethical subjectivism, egocentrism, is the basic principle of all of Kierkegaard's philosophy of existence. The ethical as the internal is inaccessible to any external scrutiny, any objective understanding. Nor is this personal actuality subject to external expression. Nothing is more disastrous for ethics than constraint on it by scientific knowledge: "The ethical is the enemy of knowledge." (6, 17, 129) Physics crushes ethics as metaphysics drives out theology. "The entire modern statistical approach to morality connives at this" (7, 202), inasmuch as it generalizes, whereas genuine ethics calls for individualization.

In the face of statistics, in the face of science, the function of ethics is to transform the human being into an individual, to make him himself. "For Kierkegaard," Bogen remarks, "not being oneself is the norm for most people...Kierkegaard is convinced that most people have not yet become individuals but only have the possibility of doing so." (38, 376, 397) (retrans. from Russian) In common language, saying that "the human being must become himself" is nonsense. And no one and nothing can or does make a human being himself. Only he himself can and must do that himself by free choice of himself, self-determination. "To be human" in the ontological sense does not by any means mean the same thing as "to be human" in the ethical sense that Kierkegaard attaches to the phrase.*

Given such a subjectivist approach to the problems of morality Kierkegaard's sharply negative attitude to Hegel's ethical views was quite inevitable. He is not content to refute these views, but denies that there is any ethics in Hegel at all; he says there is no room for an ethics in a logical system. "The Hegelian philosophy does not have any ethics." (6, 36, 145) Kierkegaard and Hegel have no common language for arguing on the ethical plane; their positions are not only incompatible, they are incommensurable. According to Hegel, it *appears*, "no kind of moral self-consciousness exists..." (16, 4, 330), inasmuch as "*morality* is the completion of the *objective* spirit..." (my italics – B.B.). (16, 3, 305) Hegel sets as his task historical knowledge of morality as logical necessity, whereas for Kierkegaard the ethical is neither historical nor logical. "The Hegelian philosophy considers the past, six thousand years of world history.... But the late Professor Hegel, when he lived, had or should have had, like every living human being, an ethical relation to future life. But nothing is known of this in the Hegelian philosophy. It follows quite simply from this that any living person who wishes to cope with his own personal life with the aid of the Hegelian philosophy will fall into the deepest confusion." (6, 36, 145)

Kierkegaard takes advantage of the circumstance that the Hegelian ethics, like all of his idealist dialectics, is turned towards the past, rather than striving towards the future; Kierkegaard's purpose is to divorce the entire ethical problematic from historical regularity, to remove morality from the sphere of socio-historical causation, since "ethical actuality is not an external historical manifestation of the personality" (6, 16, II, 287), and it is not concretized in the world-historical process. The ethical is a personal, not an historical, matter. It is not social being nor social consciousness that is the key to the ethical, but free individual choice. And it is not the human essence, immutable or transforming historically,

---

* This is how Hans Christian Andersen, whose first novel Kierkegaard criticized severely, protrayed Kierkegaard in the *Lucky Galoshes;* "The parrot can utter distinctly only one phrase, which sometimes sounds very comical: "No, we will be people!", and everything else came out just as unintelligible as the chirping of a canary." (13,1, 229)

that determines ethical "existence," but the latter, forming the personality, that determines the individual essence of each single human being, making him what he is and of what sort he is. "The desperate attempts of the unfortunate Hegelian ethics (it turns out that it exists, after all! – B.B.) to make the state the final ethical instance is an attempt, unethical to the highest degree, to limit the personality, an unethical desertion from the category of personality to the category of genus." (6, 16, II, 212) Hegel, considering morality in a world-historical perspective, does not see the trees for the wood, as Kierkegaard says. (6, 16, I, 149) It does not occur to his mind, preoccupied with himself alone, that he himself falls into the opposite extreme and does not see the wood for the trees. Going astray into the blind alley of subjectivity, he goes off the track that leads to an understanding of morality, inasmuch as not only the human race but the individual as well is a social-historical phenomenon. Neither can be understood apart from their regular interaction and interdependence.

For all its continual claims to being dialectical, Kierkegaard's ethics is antihistorical from beginning to end, and thereby undialectical. What it aims at finding out is not an historically conditioned, and therefore relative, morality, but an absolute ethics, not historically conditioned and having no historical significance, playing no role in the course of human history. The concreteness of the ethical, which Kierkegaard demands in contrast to ethical abstractions, is not embodied in historical-evolutionary concreteness but in subjective-personal diversity. Kierkegaard regards as erroneous an approach to ethics which proceeds from the assumption "that ethics finds its concretization only in the world-historical." (6, 16, I, 132) The ethical, he is convinced, not only is not indissolubly linked with the historical but is essentially anti-historical. Moral perfection is not involved in historical development but, what is more, leads to increasing alienation from the historical. The human personality, "the more it is ethically developed, the less it is concerned with the world-historical." (6, 15, I, 147) The two are processes that take place in entirely different directions, on planes that do not touch. Kierkegaard's doctrine of ethical stages has nothing in common with the history of ethics as it has been transformed in the course of social existence. The three ethical stages he sets up are not stages of the development of a form of social consciousness but three mutually exclusive aspects of the self-consciousness of the individual as such, considered outside of historical reality. The concretization of the ethical proclaimed by Kierkegaard is actually an abstraction from individualistic subjectivity, the *Ego*, and not even the *Ego* in general, at that, but *my individual Ego*.

The three ethical stages or aspects that Kierkegaard contraposes to one another are three ethical alternatives: the esthetic, ethical and religious. In his works each of them is given a vivid artistic depiction and a painstaking philosophical analysis and evaluation. The first two stages, or forms of life, two "spheres of existence," are discussed in his first major ethical work, the two-volume *Enten–Eller* (*Either–Or*, 1843). What we find there is not a chain of logical arguments and proofs but "a fireworks display of situations and inspired edifying tirades." (89, 88)

The primordial, esthetic stage is based on an immediate, sensual form of life. Here the term "esthetic" is used in the broad sense in which it was applied by Kant, the sense of "sensualism," all the things that in contradistinction to intellect and rationality relate to sense perceptions and feelings, to everything that is "feeling in general." Esthetic perception in the sense in which we usually employ the concept, and the esthetic perception linked to it, belong in the sphere of the "esthetic" in this broader sense.

On the ethical plane in which Kierkegaard employs this term, this connection of the ethical with the "esthetic" in the narrow sense of the word is conserved, since the latter is a form of immediate sensual perception and enjoyment. But the ethical essence of the "esthetic world view" is the desire for pleasures that is imbued in man, the pursuit of sensual satisfactions, the obsession with the play of the passions. On this stage which, according to Kierkegaard, is dominant in the life of the majority of people (6, 33, 6), the guideline for behavior is *carpe diem, carpe horam*, live for today, take out of the given moment everything that you can. The dissipated student days of Kierkegaard himself are the prototype of this stage.

What Kierkegaard calls the esthetic stage is known in the history of ethics as the hedonist ethic. Kierkegaard himself and many of his commentators erroneously identify it with eudaemonism and, following the false reactionary tradition, with Epicureanism. In point of fact, the eudaemonist ethics bases morality on man's desire for happiness and argues that morality, correctly understood, not only does not contradict the desire for happiness but helps in achieving it. In contrast to hedonism, eudaemonism (whose classical expression was the ethics of Epicurus, which has been slandered and distorted by ecclesiastical obscurantists for many centuries) does not in the least identify the attainment of happiness with the pursuit of sensual, physical satisfactions. On the contrary, Epicureanism is not ascetic and at the same time points out the superiority of spiritual satisfactions, which play the decisive role in achieving the highest good and happy life.

The esthetic stage, as Kierkegaard depicts it, is not an expression of eudaemonism in its best manifestations; it is typical of vulgar hedonism. According to Kierkegaard, the culminating expression of this stage is the pursuit of sexual pleasure. The esthetic stage is concentrated as the erotic stage. In it the theme is not the elevated Eros chanted by Plato, but an eroticism, symbolized for Kierkegaard by Don Juan, whom he transfers into philosophy from the musical sphere of the opera of Mozart, which he loved in the days of his youth.

A characteristic trait of the esthetic world view is its specific attitude towards time. For that world view the finite, transient instant is everything. Change of pleasures, their diversity, variation, variegation, are the constant condition of sensual satisfaction. Repetitiveness and monotony are fatal for pleasure; they contain the source of dissatisfaction. In eroticism, custom is a profanation, a degeneration of love.

Kierkegaard introduces John the Seducer in the role of the character who is the "ultra" of the esthetic stage; in contrast to Don Juan, he is not driven by greed for new erotic conquests but by a cultivated, refined sensuality, esthetic gourmandise.

This impatience with the customary and repeated, so characteristic of the esthetic stage, this cult of the unrepeatable moment, decomposes, from within, the esthetic way of perceiving the world. As Thompson put it (cf. 93, 219), the profession of being Don Juan inevitably degenerates into the Hegelian "bad infinity." Unrepeatableness is repeated and pleasure is dulled more and more, worn away, cheapened, and brings satiety, dissatisfaction, disillusionment. This dissatisfaction becomes continual and entails the bitterness of disillusionment. For on the esthetic stage man is not master of himself; invincible passions master him. "Kierkegaard's esthetic individual is entangled in the network of the passions, and yet he is not sufficiently passionate to assume mastery over his own life." (41, 262) In Kierkegaard's words, "Epicureanism is dependent on conditions beyond its control." (6, 2–3, 28).*

Doubt, reflexion, skepticism are the inevitable fruits as the esthetic stage matures. "...Happiness, unhappiness, fate, immediate excitement, disillusionment: such is the lot of the esthetic world view." (6, 16, II, 141) In Kierkegaard, the symbol of this doubt corroding the esthetic stage is Doctor Faust tempted by Mephistopheles and faced with the full keenness of the problem of the finite, transient, temporal and the infinite, intransient, eternal.

But the doubt gnawing at Faust is not yet the culminating phase of the esthetic stage. Its inevitable culmination is boredom, hopelessness,

---

* Historical Epicureanism sees the weakness of hedonism as consisting in the fact that sensual satisfactions, unlike spiritual ones, make us dependent on conditions beyond our control.

boundless desperation. "Any kind of esthetic conception of the world is desperation, and every one who lives esthetically is desperate, whether he knows it or not." (6, 2–3, 197) Despair is a "fatal disease," which overtakes every one who lives in the esthetic stage, mercilessly striking and corroding his consciousness. The symbolic figure of the man afflicted with this fatal disease is, in Kierkegaard, Ahasuerus, the "wandering Jew," condemned by pitiless fate to endless wanderings, the cares and anxiety of existence with no exit.

In total contrast to the esthetic stage which leads to self-negation, is the ethical stage, the embodiment of which for Kierkegaard is Assessor Wilhelm. If the esthetic way is the way of pleasure, the ethical way is the way of virtue, whose criterion is performance of duty. To the hedonist ethic is contrasted ethical rigorism, a way of life governed by the consciousness of responsibility, the feeling of duty. Here the norm of behavior is not immediate inclination but choice mediated by the consciousness of duty. Here man acts with respect to himself as father and mentor. "When the basic personality is employed to surmount and reinforce itself, we have the ethical view." (6, 16, II, 283) The *Ego* is transformed from an end in itself to a means to an end. The ethical man, unlike the esthetic man, becomes his own task. Ethical existence, unlike the esthetic, is not the self-gratification of the individual but the realization of the general. "The ethical as such is universal" (6, 4, 91) and requires elimination of what is individual.

The ethical stage, as presented in the second part of *Either–Or* and in *Stages on the Way of Life*, is in keeping with Kant's ethics, which may be regarded as the classical theoretical expression of this stage, to which Kierkegaard's works gave brilliant picturesque expression. "Kierkegaard takes the Kantian conception of morality as [the] highest possible expression" of what he calls the ethical stage. (91, 689) His Assessor Wilhelm upholds, in his battle agains "estheticism," a simplified version of the categorical imperative. In keeping with Kant's demand, he argues that "our affective life is required to conform to rational canons," aimed at and controlling out sensual urges, "which it does not supply from itself." (91, 693)

As in the description of the esthetic stage, the ethical stage is presented against an erotic background. Both are drawn up after the example of sex relations. While the norm for the first stage is diversity, change, inconstancy, the second stage is characterized by constancy, custom, repetition. The paradigm of the ethical existence are the marriage bonds, conjugal fidelity. "Marriage," the representative of this stage explains, "I consider to be the highest goal of individual human existence." (6, 15, 107) Whereas to the "esthete" Don Juan nothing is more foreign than marital relations based on adherence to duty, the concentrated expression of the ethical ideal could be considered to be the practice of the Jesuits in Paraguay, who rang a bell at midnight to call husbands to the fulfillment of their conjugal duty. (cf. 41, 34)

Such is the ethical alternative. Such are the two opposites, incompatible and mutually exclusive: either–or. Man is faced with a choice which determines his entire world view, his entire way of life. He must choose; he cannot help choosing. Whether he wants to or not, he will always choose his way of living. He decides and acts one way or another.

But do not hurry with your choice. Even though convinced by Assessor Wilhelm that the esthetic way is disastrous, do not hasten onto the ethical way. That is not the only alternative, and the ethical is not the highest, culminating stage on the way of life. Stop for a while at the crossroads. There are three roads before you, not two. The ethical stage is as incomplete as the esthetic. It is only a transitional stage. Kierkegaard does not rest with the formula: either–or, *tertium non datur*. Although the third choice is not given, it is set as a problem. He calls on us to travel a different, a third road.

Rejecting eudaemonism,* Kierkegaard also objects to the ethics of both Kant and Hegel.

Either–Or does not yet give a complete idea of the ethical views of its author. In it Kierkegaard "does not yet go beyond the ethical." (6, 33, 31) "It is only two acts...of the drama of existence, and not the conclusion." (51, 254) In much the same way as the second part of this book is a categorical repudiation of the esthetic stage, his later works, particularly *Fear and Trembling*, make an analogous repudiation of the ethical stage in the name of a higher ascent on the ethical ladder to the third, religious stage. "The ethical sphere is only a transitory stage... the stage of completion is the religious one...." (6, 15, 291)

The choice between the esthetic and ethical stages does not provide a solution to the problem of existence. The correct answer is not "either–or" but "neither–nor." Kierkegaard makes his way between the "Scylla of esthetic existence and the Charybdis of ethical existence" (48, 77), fighting his way through to religious ethics. In so doing the relationship among the three stages does not, contrary to what might be expected, reproduce the dialectical scheme of the Hegelian triad. It still might be possible to speak of the first two stages as thesis and antithesis, but the third is in no way a dialectical synthesis realizing the *Aufhebung*. It is not a dialectical "negation of the negation," nor an undialectical negation of

---

* Criticizing eudaemonistic ethics on the basis of a critique of the primitive hedonistic form is as silly as condemning the doctrine of Epicurus because of the objections raised by the Cyrenaic Aristippus.

the two preceding stages, as the negation of the ethics of inclination and appetite by the ethics of moral duty was. Moreover, as Price accurately observes, the passage to the subsequent stage is not a movement having the character of an evolution, but a leap based on free choice. (86, 159) The preceding stage is rejected, dismissed. The relation of the succeeding to the preceding is not here the dialectical relation of "the new" to the "old," with the new subsuming within itself the positive achievements of that which has been surpassed. What we have are alternatives, not successive stages of development. Kierkegaard's third stage does not include within itself the esthetic elements denied on the second stage, but suppresses and eradicates them even more radically. For the religious-ethical stage is nothing but an apology for suffering.

The personification of the third stage is the Abraham of the Bible, sacrificing to God his beloved only son Isaac. This image, presented in *Fear and Trembling*, brilliantly shows the contrast between the religious-ethical and the ethical stages. From the standpoint of the latter, Abraham's action calls for decisive condemnation as immoral, a violation of family and human duty, let alone natural inclinations. From the ethical point of view, what we have here is not merely an immoral, brutal breach of moral duty, but a monstrous crime. Abraham's motive is devoid of any moral or rational ground. His only motive is devoid of any moral or rational ground. His only motive is blind obedience to the mandate of God. What seems, by a human criterion, to be a criminal homicide appears on a religious evaluation as an act pleasing to God, the offering of a sacrifice. Duty to humanity yields to duty to God. The criterion of good and evil is transformed into its opposite. If on the ethical stage family bonds are the model of morality, on the religious stage they become a hindrance that has to be removed. In this way the religious-ethical stage serves Kierkegaard as justification for his own breach of the vow of fidelity given to Regina; his renunciation of her is assimilated to a sacrifice in the name of a religious duty to whose fulfillment the author of *Fear and Trembling* devoted his life.

The religious stage signifies "teleological renunciation of the moral" (4, 57); in point of fact, it is anti-ethical. Kierkegaard himself calls it "extraordinarily paradoxical." For in order to be religious it is necessary to break with morality. We must agree with Blanshard when he says that, as Kierkegaardian fideist super-truth undermines truth, his religious ethics denies moral values. (cf. 36, 13-14) The example of Abraham adduced by Kierkegaard is convincing testimony that "human being and morally responsible existence (as Kierkegaard calls it – B.B.) are mutually exclusive." (63, 53) "Christianity in the New Testament signifies: love God in hatred towards man, in hatred towards self and therefore towards other people as well, in hatred towards father and mother, towards one's own offspring, towards one's wife, etc...." (6, 34, 182) Obviously, the religious-ethical stage is diametrically opposed to the Kantian categorical imperative: Kierkegaard leaves no room either for the principle of universal legislation or for responsibility with reference to every man as an end; he transfers moral norms to the sphere of the irrational. (cf. 91, 689 and 700) From the standpoint of the religious stage, ethics as such, pretending to autonomy and secularization, represents a danger to religion, containing and limiting its absolute, indisputable claims and entering into irreconcilable conflict with it. It is not only, not even particularly, traditional every-day morality that is involved, the morality that Kierkegaard had in mind when he asked ironically: " 'Did the Apostle Paul hold any position?' No, Paul had no position of any kind. 'Then did he make a great deal of money in some other way?' No, he did not make any money. 'But was he married at least?' No, he was not married. 'But in that case Paul was not a responsible person!' No, to be sure, Paul was not a responsible person." (6, 34, 202) What is at issue is not only criteria of this sort but the ethical concept of duty, of terrestrial, human, moral criterial in general.

As on the ethical stage, the criterion of morality has a formal character on the religious stage too, so that not the content and function of the act are determined but its motivation. But whereas in Kant this formal criterion is constituted by being conditioned by an a priori categorical imperative ("you must because you should"), in Kierkegaard it is conditioned by free choice: not what is chosen but how it is chosen, not what is decided but "the determination to decide." The example of Abraham shows how such a choice is determined in the face of moral duty.

In contrast to rigoristic ethics, which requires unequivocal obedience to duty, the morality based on freedom of choice presupposes alternance, the rivalry of different motives and impulses. Here "the good in general is impossible to define. The good is freedom. The difference between good and evil exists only for freedom and in freedom...." (6, 11–12, 114) "There is no difference between good and evil until that difference is realized thanks to freedom." (6, 11–12, 52) The good is thus constituted by my choice, which can be determined by nothing other than my freedom. It does not admit of necessity and is nothing but the urge "to be oneself." (6, 10, 13) In choosing, man chooses himself, becomes a person. The watchword of Socrates, "Know thyself!" gives way to Kierkegaard's voluntaristic, "Choose thyself!" And this choice, this decision predetermines what is good, as my conviction predetermines what is truth. Does this not lead Kierkegaard to ethical nihilism, as

Blanshard holds (36, 10), in the same way as "the truth for me" leads inevitably to fideism? And is not the popularity of his religious ethics in American schools of theology a real anomaly? (35, 12) We shall consider the answer to this question after further acquaintance with Kierkegaard's view.

Whatever the formal criterion may be that Kierkegaard sets up, it cannot avoid the question of the content of choice. Choice presupposes an alternative. Between what? The alternative posed in *Either–Or*, we saw, faces us with the choice between hedonism and rigorism, duty and the ethics of impulse. But beyond this alternative lies the choice between egoism and altruism, love of self and love of humanity, the particular and the general. The religious-ethical stage escapes from the initial alternative, but is it capable of escaping the dilemma lying behind that alternative? If choice presupposes responsibility, is it responsibility only to oneself or to people, family, nation, society, humanity?

Here and there we find in Kierkegaard an answer to this question, "going beyond" the dilemma: "No individual is as indifferent to the history of the race as the race is to any individual." "...The entire race participates in the individual, and the individual in the entire race." (6, 11–12, 26)

But isolated statements of this sort in Kierkegaard are submerged and dissolved in the flood of egocentrism that pervades his works. "What I am interested in in this regard," he writes with reference to his ethical interests, "is myself." (6, 11–12, 16) Kierkegaard calls for "unbounded concentration on self," seeing therein "the highest task" faced by every human being. "To be an individual personality...is the unique true and highest calling of man and thereby higher than any other vocation...." (6, 16, I, 739) "For Socratic examination, every separate human being is the focus for himself, and all the world becomes a focus only in relation to him." (6, 10, 9) "...Every one has to save himself and be satisfied with that...." (6, 16, 41) Such is the leitmotif repeated in endless variations in Kierkegaard's religious-ethical fugue.

Now what does the introverted self-absorbed individual find in himself, what does he discover in the bowels of his *Ego*, what kind of essence of existence is revealed to him?

The philosophy of existence is shot through with profound pessimism. Man is doomed to suffering. Life is a vale of tears. To live means to suffer. How blind, how invincibly deluded are people in the grasp of optimism, "these thousands and thousands living in the blessed illusion that life is a joy...." (7, 599) Kierkegaard looks at life with other eyes. Man is cast, as into a pit, into an alien and dismal world. "All being frightens me," he writes in his *Diary* on May 12, 1839, "everything in it is incomprehensible to me, and I myself most of all; for me, all being is poisoned, and I myself most of all. Great, unbounded is my suffering...." (7, 118–119)

While the fundamental category of esthetic existence is "enjoyment," and of ethical existence, "duty," on the religious stage the fundamental category of existence is "suffering." Although existence is not free from suffering even on the first two stages, still "in the esthetic and the ethical suffering is something fortuitous, which can or cannot occur. It is different in the religious sphere...." (6, 16, I, 283) Upon reaching this sphere man is plunged into suffering that overpowers him. The religious man is a suffering man. "With the elimination of suffering the religious life is eliminated as well." (6, 16, II, 155)

However, the distinguishing characteristic of this doctrine is not that suffering is regarded as the universal form of existence, its attribute as it were, but its attitude towards suffering. Suffering is not merely real and inevitable, but proper and necessary. It should be not only endured but desired. "Blessings on suffering...", Kierkegaard exclaims. (cited from 50, 59) Here we see the basic opposition between the religious-ethical stage and the esthetic stage, which resents suffering, resists it without truce and is conquered by it.

Kierkegaard asserts that if we are not merely reconciled to suffering but love it, we arrive at a level of existence which rises above all unhappiness and surpasses all happiness (cf. 6, 16, II, 152) In that case, he concludes, the object is not to avoid suffering and make life easier, but to complicate life and make it more difficult, to hinder one's own happiness and that of others in every way (cf. 6, 16, I, 177), leading us to live "breathing suffering." (6, 16, II, 144) Transforming suffering into a blessing, we overcome the antimony of happiness and unhappiness. Here choice, which determines the moral norm, is directed at the attitude towards suffering. A positive attitude is set up as against the negative attitude characteristic of the esthetic stage.

Kierkegaard's apology for suffering puts him outside the ranks of the theologians who for centuries strove with all their might to found a theodicy, to justify God for the evil, injustice and suffering that prevail in the world. Kierkegaard differs from the authors of theodicies who denied the reality of evil in the world and appealed to the imperfection of human reason, assuring us that we live in the best of all possible worlds and trying in every way to rehabilitate God's infinite power, wisdom and goodness; Kierkegaard does not attempt to deny that the world is full of evil and suffering. God does not need to be justified to man, and faith in him does not permit of critical appraisal of his will. Faith demands submission to the creator of all that is, as it is. Faith in

God does not permit of doubt and cannot be shaken by anything. And "even if the whole world bursts and all the elements are confounded, thou shalt believe." (6, 17, 139)

Complete fideism is incompatible with theodicy. Our reason cannot be either prosecutor or defense attorney or still less judge of the All-Highest. Love of God must be unconditional. No sufferings, deprivations or adversity, no trials and tribulations can shake or diminish it. For Kierkegaard, the Biblical myth of long-suffering Job is the paradigm of such a love. For, in endowing man with freedom of choice (and therewith of choice of his attitude towards suffering), did not God endow him with the greatest of gifts? "The entire question of the relation of the divine goodness and omnipotence to evil can be solved quite simply, if you will...: the highest thing that can in general be done for any being is to make him free." (7, 239) And once that being is free, i.e. free to live as he pleases, no claims against his creator can be allowed. For with correct choice, suffering itself becomes the source of good and bliss.

But let us penetrate further into the murky labyrinth of the Kierkegaardian cogitations. Man, endowed with freedom by the creator, has made his choice, misusing his freedom. Adam committed the original sin, using his freedom for the fall. This "leap" from innocence into sinfulness placed a heavy burden on the shoulders of all humankind. From that time on all of us are sinners. Sin weighs down all of the human race, all of us descendants of Adam. Why that is so is not accessible to rational knowledge; "no science can give an explanation of sin." (6, 11–12, 78) Nonetheless, "sin is the decisive expression of religious existence... the decisive point of departure..." (6, 16, I, 262) All existence goes forward marked by guilt. The feeling of guilt, conditioned by man's sinfulness, is permanent, cannot be removed or eliminated; it deepens human suffering. Only by consciousness of guilt is the existent being plunged into genuine suffering and woe. Guilt, in Kierkegaard's words, is "the *decisive* expression of the existential pathos." (6, 16, II, 235)

In whose eyes is man guilty? Against whom has he transgressed? Not against other people. Sin is not an antisocial action; it is not violation of the norms of social conduct. Man is guilty before God. Tasting the forbidden fruit, Adam made use of the freedom given him to violate the divine command. Original sin and the sacrifice of Isaac are the two poles of religious morality: evil and good. Here duty is understood on the basis of an entirely different criterion than on the ethical stage. Sin is not an ethical but a religious category. Here the individual is contraposed not to the general but to the absolute. Sin is not defined by the relations among people, which is the case with the ethical relation, but by the relationship of man to God, who does not participate in inter-human relationships. At this point we come close to an explanation of what is really the most important consideration, decisive for understanding of the difference in principle in the character of the religious stage of existence advocated by Kierkegaard from that of the ethical stage he excludes and rejects. From this point of view the formula of anthropological humanism put forward by Feuerbach, according to which "man becomes God in his relationship to another man," is to Kierkegaard only "empty chatter," (6, 10, 99), and not in any way a religious ethics.

Another fundamental existentialist category, along with freedom, suffering, sin and guilt, is dread; it is also one of the integral forms, or attributes, of human existence. Dread forms an indissoluble unity with sin, suffering and freedom. Kierkegaard expressly stipulates that "dread," in his acceptation, should not be identified with "fear." It is not the fear of some definite danger threatening the person. Dread is a feeling without an object; it overpowers a person; it is dread of "nothing," alarm, uneasiness. "Dread," by Kierkegaard's definition, "is the relation of freedom to guilt." (6, 11-12, 109) True dread is the sinner's dread before God. It is not a base feeling nor an animal instinct, but a sign of perfection of human nature: "He who has learned to dread really, has learned the highest of matters." (6, 11-12, 161) Like suffering, dread is the motive force of the religious consciousness. It has its source in faith and inculcates faith. "Abolish the consciousness of dread," Kierkegaard says, "and you may as well close the churches and turn them into dance halls." (6, 4, 221) There is a striking concurrence here between Kierkegaard's conception of the psychology of the religious consciousness and Feuerbach's analysis of the emotional roots of religious faith. Truly, extremes meet. The fanatical apologist for religion confirms the diagnosis made by the atheist.

The focal point of dread is the fear of death. "What is a human being afraid of more than anything else? In all likelihood, death...." (5, X12, A422) Fear of death accompanies man, like a shadow, all the way through life. Death is not that which crowns life but that which hangs over it, condemned as it is from the day of its birth. Man's life is "a life to death." "It seems to me," an entry in the *Diary* in 1837 runs, "as though I were a galley-slave under sentence of death; at every instant, with every movement of life, my chain gives a ringing sound and everything pales before the face of death – *and this takes place every minute.*" (7, 85) Since the beginning of time the fear of death has been a favorite religious theme and a most effective means of influence in the mouths of clerical preachers. Kierkegaard continues this tradition, trying to get the maximum psychological effect out of exhortations on "what death is and what it is for the living, how the idea of it should transform the entire life of every man...." (6, 16, I, 159) All men are mortal, I am a man, therefore I am mortal, unavoidably sentenced to death – this sounds like an echo in his consciousness at every step along the path of a man's life. And death is not a distant prospect for him. "...The possibility of death exists at every moment." (6, 16, I, 74) Its inevitability is linked with the indeterminateness of the mortal hour. It is hidden around every corner; it constantly threatens with its unexpectedness. And this combination reinforces the fear of death even more, making it the constant fellow-traveller of life.

Following Kierkegaard, we have now arrived at a turning point in his pessimistic cogitations. If life is nothing but suffering, dread, guilt, then is there any sense to it? Is attachment to life justified? Is not human existence meaningless? Is not all the time man spends on earth a waste of time? For time is "man's worst enemy." Would it not be better to "kill time"? By committing suicide, "I kill time with this one shot." (7, 199) Is not all life, after all, an empty and trivial "child's play?" (6, 11–12, 95) Kierkegaard's answer to these questions is not based on the will to live nor on love and attachment to existence, but on estrangement from life and contempt for existence. If life has no values, then does it matter how one lives? Kierkegaard remarks, with bitter irony: "Marry, and you will be sorry for it; don't marry, and you will be sorry for that too: whether you marry or not, you will be sorry in either case.... Hang yourself, and you will be sorry for it; don't hang yourself, and you will be sorry for that too: you will be sorry in either case. That, gentlemen, is the resumé of all the wisdom of life...." (6, 1, 41–42) "Status, knowledge, glory, friendship, pleasure and good – all that is only wind and smoke, or, to say it more truly, all that is nothing," are verses of Pellison that he places as epigraph to the first part of *Either–Or*. "Good health, feeling good, is a far greater danger than wealth, power, glory." (7, 404)

Estrangement from earthly goods, contempt for all finite, earthly interests, are not indifference or apathy, but a choice, a decision, taken by Kierkegaard and recommended by him. "The first true expression of a relation to the abolute goal is renunciation of everything...." (6, 16, II, 111) Monasticism and asceticism are inadequate for the purpose; what is decisive is not the outward manifestation but the inner relationship. The words of the Apostle Paul: "My kingdom is not of this world," are inscribed on the existentialist banner of Kierkegaard. (6, 34, 27) "Christian doctrine proclaims that suffering is a blessing, that denial of self is a blessing, that renunciation of the world is a blessing. And in that is the heart of that doctrine." (5, XV, A666) We shall return to the question of how this preachment of denial of self accords with Kierkegaard's egocentrism. However that may be, the feeling that inspired his entire attitude towards life sounds with exceptional force of expression in the words of his last entry in his *Diary* (September 25, 1855): "The purpose of life is to bring oneself to the highest degree of *tedium vitae*." Such is the final sentence passed by Kierkegaard on human existence. Nonetheless, despair is not his final word.

Working his way, in the pages of his works, along the thorny path of inextricable suffering, dread, fearful freedom, guilt that is not guilty of anything, and contempt for life, Kierkegaard comes to the edge of the abyss. He comes there and halts. No, one must not fall into despair! Not end life. Despair is not only a weakness but a sin. In and of itself, life is aimless and meaningless. "Suffer, bear suffering, go towards death. But suffering is not an end." (6, 16, II, 311) Life's suffering must be given a meaning, making it a means to an end. After arriving at contempt for life, one must life to expiate guilt, working out in life atonement for sin. Kierkegaard makes a virtue of necessity. "The Christian is no masochist..since suffering is a means and a springboard forward, rather than an end in itself." (41, 222)

Accounting despair as the end result of *thought*, Kierkegaard contraposes faith to thinking. His final alternative is: either faith or despair. He rejects despair as lack of faith, lack of faith in salvation. As in the sphere of knowledge, fideism asserts its rights in the sphere of morality. Life, full of suffering, acquires a meaning and justification as the way to salvation through atonement. Suffering is the dear price at which God Almighty sells man the salvation to come.

If reason leads to despair, faith saves us from it: such is the basic principle of religious existentialism. If reason convinces us there is no hope, faith gives us hope and consolation. Faith is the only consolation, "the only means against weak-nerved impatience." (6, 36, 190) This hope is irrational. It is not based on rational inferences. It cannot be proved. In Kierkegaard, we might say, Hope is the daughter of Faith and not of Wisdom. We must have faith in this hope, even if it is hopeless: that is the next paradox of the religious stage. "When the poor worker falls in love with the princess and has faith in her love for him, what then would be the humblest way of his convincing himself of that?" (6, 16, II, 202) He can have no other pretensions. His faith warms him.

Hope for what? For the immortality of the soul. Over against life, which is transitory, temporal suffering, stands eternal bliss. Man is at a crossroads, with two roads before him. One or the other: either temporal, earthly life, dread and suffering, "or contempt for the earthly, Christianity preaching sacrifice and suffering" (6, 27–29, 166), as the way to eternal bliss in the beyond. Faith converts suffering into an act of expiation; it frees from the fear of death. Death is transformed into deliverance, becomes a hope. And if, "speaking humanly, death is the very last thing and, speaking humanly, there is hope only as long as there is life, on the Christian view, death is not at all the last thing...and, on the Christian view, there is infinitely more hope in death than, speaking humanly, there is not only in life but in life in full health and strength." (cited from 42, 66) Thus, pessimism is "surmounted" by an apology for death. The fear of death gives way to an expectation of it as a rapturous hope, as deliverance. "Death is the universal good fortune of all men...." (6, 1, 200) The leap from morality to religion that Kierkegaard preaches is, in the literal sense of the phrase, a *salto mortale*, which delivers us from despair, dread and suffering. The fear of death is not removed by contempt for death but by contempt for life, by the wish for death, by worship of it. Such is the pathological finale of pathetic fideism.

Following on this is the unchecked mystique of the immortality of the soul and bliss beyond the grave. But we will spare the reader and limit ourselves to citing only a few of his utterances, which speak for themselves and require no commentary. "...Is it completely certain," he asks, "that eternal bliss awaits us?" The answer to this question places us at "an abyss across which reason cannot go...." But that does not change matters, "since I," Kierkegaard concedes, "do not in any way intend to prove that eternal bliss exists...." (6, 16, II, 129–132) The essential thing is that "the question of immortality is in essence not a scientific question at all.... Objectively, this question does not admit of any answer.... Immortality is the most passionate of needs, in which the subjectivity is interested, and it is precisely in that interest that the proof consists." (6, 16, I, 164) Who is there that will not be convinced by this advertisement? Here Kierkegaard is betrayed by his famous irony. "...Purely metaphysically, no man is immortal and there is no assurance of his immortality." (6, 11–12, 160) "This problem is not a logical problem at all; what does logical thought have in common with the ultrapathetic (the question of eternal bliss)?" (6, 16, II, 66) And that which cannot be proved cannot be refuted either, is that not so? But "I, John Climacus (Kierkegaard's pseudonym in the *Philosophical Sketches* – B.B.)...have faith that a higher bliss awaits me, eternal happiness.... And I have heard that Christianity is recommended as the condition for attaining to that bliss!"

Such is the "absolutely only hope" that Kierkegaard proposes to man, a "hopeless hope." (cf. 6, 11, 69) "...If the holy world is not able to find the way to the truth, glory to the madman who evokes a golden dream for mankind!" his followers might cry.*

On this stage, what are the interrelations of egocentrism, theocentrism and anthropocentrism? What, as Kierkegaard himself asks, is "the Archimedean point" of human existence: love for self, for God or for people? Responsibility for what determines moral valuations and norms?

Rohde thinks that "Kierkegaard was an individualist to the extreme of its consequences...." (89, 158) Tilsch and Bogen do not consider him an individualist. (cf. 67, 6, 160; 38, 375) Kierkegaard himself makes statements enough that testify to his extreme individualism. "If the personality," he writes, "is absolute, then it in itself is that Archimedean point from which the world can be moved." (6, 2, 287) "There is so much that attests that Christianity does not presuppose anything human," we read in his *Diary*. "There is something, however, that it clearly presupposes, namely self-love...." (7, 122) "The personality is the decisive Christian category" (6, 10, 95), Kierkegaard repeats constantly.

But the egocentrism and extreme individualism of Kierkegaard's "Individual" is essentially different from the atheistic egocentrism of Stirner's "Individual." The difference is so great that it leads many students of Kierkegaard to speak of his theocentrism, despite the fact that Kierkegaard himself speaks scornfully of "the theocentric nineteenth century." (6, 16, II, 101)

What was his attitude towards the dignity and freedom of man, of the human personality that he sings of and glorifies in every way? For all that man, as we know, is made in the likeness and form of God, there is an absolute qualitative difference between them, to which Kierkegaard calls attention on every occasion that arises. "The entire confusion of modern times is based on the fact that people wanted to do away with the qualitative chasm that separates God and man" (7, 285), who are incommensurable and incomparable. On one side of this charm is a perfect omnipotent being, and on the other "an infinitely little, vanishingly imperceptible atom" (6, 16, II, 336), an insignificant being incapable of anything. (cf. 6, 16, II, 88)

How is the cult of the *Ego* to be reconciled with disdain for human insignificance? The *Ego*, it appears, is possessed of dignity and is an end in itself only by the grace of God, and in its devotion to the All-Highest. In fact, the introverted personality, absorbed in itself, must find itself

---

* This is "the most frightful, most unbearable book that was ever printed," I. S. Turgenev wrote to Pauline Viardot (June 20, 1859) after reading Pascal's *Pensées*. "He tramples on everything that man holds dear, and throws us to the ground, into the mud, and then, to console you, offers us a religion which reason (the reason of Pascal himself) can not but reject, but which the heart must accept submissively." This description applies fully to Kierkegaard's conception of the religious stage, as well.

not in itself but in God. The relationship to God makes the human being human. The measure of the *Ego* is always what the *Ego* is before God. "For the greatness of man depends only and exclusively on the energy of the relationship to God in himself...." (6, 11–12, 113) "Inwardness *(Innerlichkeit)*," runs a fundamental formula of Kierkegaard's, "is the relationship of the personality to itself before God." (6, 16, II, 144) And "the relationship of the personality to the eternal determines what the nature of his existence is, and not vice versa." (6, 16, II, 286) Without its relationship to God, without worship of him, without submission and obedience to him, the personality is not a personality.

On the one hand is the abstract personality, divorced from history, from nature, from society; on the other is God, elevated above history and nature: that is Kierkegaard's duality in unity. Is it egocentrism? Yes, "the Individual is the category on which the cause of Christianity stands and with which it falls.... The Individual is unique in all the world, unique before God." (6, 33, 117) Man, for whom there is nothing except himself and God is a man for whom there is nothing except himself. He exists for God insofar as God exists for him. "I chose the Absolute. But what is the Absolute? It is myself in my eternal value." (7, 2, 231) Underneath the thick religious coloration egocentrism continues to be what it is: egocentrism robed in mysticism. The motive force of religious faith is "the infinitely passionate interest (of the personality) in its eternal bliss." (6, 16, I, 49) Kierkegaardian love for God is nothing more than maximal love for self, purchased at the price of disdain for life and people.

Tulstrup called Kierkegaard's conception "theanthropic." (68, 316) It should rather be called "theegotistic," since it is not humanity but the *Ego*, divorced from other people, that is for Kierkegaard the other end of the "*Ego*-God" axis. For, according to Kierkegaard, "every subject becomes for *himself* the very opposite of everything general whatsoever." (6, 16, I, 158) What Kierkegaard calls "the religious ethic," putting the *Ego* face to face with God, sets him with his back to people. "All thy efforts should not have any significance at all for any other man." (6, 16, I, 127) For, "the highest demand of Christian ethics is to live face to face with oneself under the eyes of God, never caring about others...." (50, 171) Even some Christian students of his doctrine (Paton, Garelick) were offended by the egoism of his "love for God" as being "inconsistent with Christianity" and "actually the antithesis to religion." But does not this fideism, carried to its utter limits, disclose the innermost tendency concealed in the core of every religion? For even the religious preachment of love of one's neighbor presupposes love for oneself, as Kierkegaard remarks in this connection (cf. 7, 122).

But does not the Christian ethic preached by Kierkegaard refute itself? Do not its conclusions deny its own premises? The cornerstone of this entire ethical structure was the God-given freedom of the will, and its moral criterion was freedom of choice, moral self-determination. But this freedom, it turns out, is realized under strict, unrelenting supervision, under the unblinking gaze of the Lord God. Is there much left of that self-determination if "a religions coloration...is given the ethical category of choice of self..." (6, 16, I, 262), when "every personality properly and essentially finds the ethical only in itself, inasmuch as the ethical is the personality's accord with God"? (6, 16, I, 145) "And what is duty then? Duty is simply the expression of the will of God." (6, 4, 64) Is not man's freedom, which determines morality, paradoxical if it is directly proportional to his dependence on God, corresponds to the will of Providence? And in that case who is the legislator of morality? The *Ego* for itself, as should be expected, starting with the *premises* of the Kierkegaardian ethic? Not at all, his *conclusions* declare: "There is not a single law here that I set for myself as a maxim; here there is only the law given me from above." (7, 443) In the last analysis, the Archimedian point from which the whole world can be moved turns out to be not the *Ego* but that which "must be outside the world, beyond the bounds of space and time." (8, 1, 21) Here lies the paradox (which is equivalent to the absurd, in Kierkegaard's terminology, and therefore the truth) of "theocentric egocentrism:" to be one's self means to be obedient to God's will, but God's will is precisely such as you chose it by your own will in the sight of the unseen and unknowable God.... That in essence is the Kierkegaardian "categorical imperative."

Kierkegaard's doctrine is ethical nihilism. What Kierkegaard calls "Christian ethics,"* is actually anti-ethics, just as his dialectics, as we saw, is anti-dialectics.

Did Kierkegaard found "an entirely new ethic, which is not determined by the relation of the individual to the common lot, but by the relation of the individual to the paradox of faith"? (56, 148) Ethics is a system of the norms and valuations of man as a social being, and what Kierkegaard proposes is not an ethics. He rejects the ethical stage of the way of life just as metaphysically, absolutely, as he does the esthetic. Where Kant admits faith in God in the name of morality as practical reason, Kierkegaard's "paradox of faith" breaks with ethics, which, in his words, "ignoring sin, becomes a 'thoroughly trivial' science." (6, 16, I, 112) His assertion that "when we forget what it means to exist religiously,

---

* As opposed to other, lower religions ("religion A"), Kierkegaard calls Christianity, as the higher religion, "religion B." His religious-ethical doctrine corresponds to the latter.

we also forget what it means to exist humanly," (6, 16, I, 244) is in crying contradiction with the actual content of his precepts. The paradigm of Abraham is a clear illustration of the antithesis of religion and morality that reigns in his doctrine. If, as Kierkegaard asserts, "the ethical culminating point of everything is immortality, and without it the ethical is merely habits and customs" (6, 16, I, 166), if human life on earth is only "the life of a fish on dry land," (57, 120), then all ethical problems lose any meaning and significance. Kierkegaard's efforts to smother ethics in religion, to dissolve morality in the hopeless hope for eternal bliss, involuntarily discloses what the religious *Weltanschauung*, which presents itself as the "bulwark of morality," so carefully covers up.

The basic task of Kierkegaard's activity throughout his life is the apology for Christianity, as he understands it. "No epoch can stand up without religion," he exclaims. (6, 36, 5) His "intention from first to last was religious, that is, to recommend the religious as the only answer to the human situation...." (86, 24) Not religion as morality but religion instead of morality is the essence of what he calls the religious stage on the road of life. This stage purports to *carry* man *away* "beyond good and evil." We shall see in the next chapter where it actually *leads* him.

The idea put forward by Hume in the *Dialogues on Natural Religion* and directed against religion, to the effect that the sources of faith are dread and suffering, was used by Kierkegaard to prove the value of religion. He agrees with Feuerbach's position that "the Christian religion is a religion of suffering." (24, 2, 94) Making reference to the *Essence of Christianity*, he calls attention to the fact that even such an opponent of Christianity as Feuerbach "says that religious (and above all, Christian) existence is an unbroken history of sufferings." (6, 15, 490). But Ludwig Feuerbach was not acquainted with the literary work of Kierkegaard, which provided such clear and convincing confirmation of his analysis of the emotional roots and psychological nature of religious consciousness. Kierkegaard's religious fanaticism also demonstrates, with the utmost expressiveness, the psychological mechanism of religious faith, which exercises undivided sway over the human mind and feelings. But Kierkegaard turns the edge of the emotional conception of religion in the opposite direction from that given it by Hume and Feuerbach. In his words, "Börne, Heine, Feuerbach... as a rule understand religion very well, i.e. they very definitely know that they want to have nothing to do with it." (6, 15, 482) For his part, Kierkegaard devoted all his passion and literary mastery to proving that "to be shaken...is the universal basis of all religiosity" (6, 36, 129), and applied the results of the opponents of religion to defending it. If man is condemned to suffering, from which only death brings deliverance, if all life is cheerless repentance and atonement for sin, then he has no other hope, no consolation, except unreasoning faith in the immortality of the soul and eternal bliss. The psychology of religious faith is employed in an apology for it. This requires not not only contempt for life but also contempt for *rational* life, contempt for reason, the divorce and isolation of faith from reason. Faith at all costs.

The narcotic, hallucinatory function of religious faith appears in Kierkegaard with matchless vividness, expressiveness and impressiveness, beyond any theologican before him, it may well be. Even Tertullian could not dream of a better disciple than Kierkegaard.

CHAPTER VII

A SPY IN THE SERVICE OF THE LORD

That was how Kierkegaard defined his historical mission.

In the first half of last century Denmark was a "philosophical province" of Prussia in the theoretical field; in the sphere of international relations in the period of the Napoleonic wars it was isolated from the entire anti-French coalition. Kierkegaard's youth was passed in the gloomy period of Frederick VI's reign. Feudal reaction ruled in the country. A seven-year war led to a crushing English bombardment of Copenhagen which reduced the Danish capital to ruins, annihilated the Danish fleet and brought about the bankruptcy of the government. By the treaty of Kiel in 1814 Norway was taken from Denmark. Capitalist industrialization of the country, which had not up to then experienced the industrial revolution, only began in the 1820s (the first railroad was built only in 1847). In the 1830s, under the influence of the revolutionary events in France, the beginnings of a liberal bourgeois movement were seen. A constitutional convention of the orders was convened. Christian VIII, who ascended the throne in 1839, permitted the spread of bourgeois-liberal illusions. A project for a constitutional monarchy began to be worked out. In 1848 a national liberation uprising flared up in Schleswig-Holstein, leading to a three-year war with Prussia. Even before the signing of the treaty of peace in Berlin the new Danish monarch, Frederick VII, ratified the 1849 constitution which transformed the absolute monarchy into a constitutional one. The political influence of Germany on Denmark grew stronger after the revolutionary events of 1848. "The Danes," Engels wrote in an article on "The Danish-Prussian Armistice" in the *Neue Rheinische Zeitung*, "are a nation which is in the most unlimited commercial, industrial, political and literary dependence on Germany. It is well known that the actual capital of Denmark is not Copenhagen but Hamburg...." (2, 5, 420) In a letter to Marx he gave the following description of the position of Denmark at that time: "Such a degree of moral poverty, guild and caste narrowness, no longer exists anywhere else." (2, 27, 70)

This was the unpromising historical scene against the background of which the "individual" philosopher was born, lived, worked and died. There were then sufficient grounds for Kierkegaard's bitter irony.

"...Beyond a doubt," says Sartre, "Kierkegaard was basically conditioned by the historical milieu; his disdain for the masses and his aristocratic beliefs are indubitable...in his social origins and political positions (for example, his sympathy for absolute monarchy), but also, although masked, this conditioning crops out everywhere and clearly underlies his ethical and religious positions...." But, Sartre adds, this general socio-historical conditioning "cannot be taken *as fundamental*...." (68, 52-53) In our opinion, this is precisely what should be taken *as fundamental*, even though only as fundamental. Socio-historical conditions are the necessary, although in and of themselves not sufficient, basis for explaining the origin and the historical role of his philosophy. The general, of course, does not exist without the specific and individual, but, despite the conviction of Kierkegaard himself, the individual likewise does not exist without the general, which acts as the basis which is refracted through the prism of the creative individuality, and in this case through an extremely fragmented psychological prism.

Of decisive importance for understanding the socio-political function of Kierkegaard's whole philosophy is the basic tendency of his religious-ethical doctrine to despise the world, to hold earthly life in contempt, to contrapose eternal bliss to temporal suffering. Kierkegaard brings his reader to the brink of despair and places him before a choice of alternatives: either unbounded suffering or unthinking faith; either worldly doom or recompense in the beyond, and *tertium non datur*. This alternative presupposes not only indifference to but loathing for the earthly sphere and, thereby, for socio-political activity above all. "Being incapable of embarking on such tasks as the future of all of mankind, or whatever else the demands of the time might be, I tried my best to concentrate on myself." (6, 15, 367) Social reconstruction, revolutions, political transformations – not, that is not where his thoughts, hopes and dreams were directed. "My kingdom is not of this world...." The seven-year war, the three-year war, with all their pressures and miseries – so what? "It seems to me that even in the horrors of bloody war there is something human as compared with this diplomatic peace...." (6, 17, II, 48) The revolutionary movements of 1830 and 1848 evoked only indignation in him, and liberal reforms–profound disdain. "*In essence*," Kierkegaard decrees, "there are only two parties between which a choice has to be made: either-or!... *Either* obedience to God...staying with God against people...*or* going with people against God.... For there is a struggle between the people and God, a war to the death...." (7, 504-505)

It would seem that posing the question in this way would lead to political indifferentism, would call for being apolitical. One might think that the religious self-consciousness is contraposed here to *all* political activity, to interest in politics in general. Many of Kierkegaard's statements are as it were predesignated for such a conclusion. The spirit of the time, when politics dominates everywhere, when "the entire understanding of people is so decidedly directed towards the earthly, the political, the national" (6, 33, 154), is contraposed to the sacred spirit, the spirit of God. The believer, who aims not at the temporal but at the eternal, has no concern with political squabbles, which only distract the attention of contemporaries from the All-Highest. Let the consciousness of the believer not be sullied with the finite, the relative, the transitory, "let him concern himself less with the external, but rather think of the highest goods, of the spiritual world, of the salvation of his soul...." (6, 16, II, 216)

Kierkegaard is far from any thought of founding a political party of his own or of joining any party: "I have not the slightest inclination to be a member of a party." (6, 16, II, 333) What has politics in common with "eternal truth"? "Politics begins on earth and remains on earth" (33, 96), while religion relates all our hopes and ideals to the world beyond, and hence views the political rat-race with irony. "Relationship to God is the only thing that has significance." (7, 305) Disdain for politics is a direct and inevitable conclusion from disdain for the world. And Kierkegaard preaches that conclusion stubbornly, insistently. The *Ego*, as soul, he declares in the *Edifying Discourses* of 1844, attains to itself not through its relation to this world, not through knowledge, experience, hope, etc., regardless of whether all that is affirmative or negative in character, but through immersion in love for God. (cf. 57, 71) And this disdain for the world of politics takes on concrete form: "Do not fear the world, poverty, sorrow, disease, need, vicissitudes and human injustice...but fear yourself, fear what might kill faith...." (26, 72) Die to the world, he calls out, to this "base, corrupt, evil world, fit only for rogues and scoundrels." (6, 34, 310) No concern with worldly matters. Not the slightest attempt to change the world. Not a word calling for struggle against the evil and injustice prevailing in the world. "And so I sit here. On the outside, everything is in motion, everyone is agitated by the idea of nationality.... But I sit in my quiet little room (soon they will denounce me for my indifference to the national cause); I know only one danger – the menace to religiousness." (cited from 57, 139) God estranges from the world, shuts man up within himself. "To live in the eyes of God" is nothing other than to live alone with oneself. "I," says the young Kierkegaard, "have grown into the divine, so to speak, am so inseparably linked to it that all the world may go to wrack and ruin." (7, 45)

Contempt for the world cannot but grow into contempt for people, for the human race, for mankind. "Speaking humanly, God is man's worst enemy, thy mortal enemy," Kierkegaard exclaims in one issue of his periodical *The Moment*. (6, 34, 175) The introverted personality, existing in subjectivistic self-isolation, is foreign to all that is sociable or social. Union with God can only be attained by despising the human race, not by joining it. The religious ethic is unsocial, antisocial. "...The greater the ethical development, the less time is left for the universal-historical." (6, 16, I, 152) Here are the reflections of the "ethically highly-developed personality" on the occasion of a cholera epidemic: "The significance of cholera is that it teaches people that they are personalities, something that is not done either by war or other misfortunes, which rather unite them, whereas the plague splits them up into individuals." (cited from 50, 194) Is it possible, after this, to maintain, as Collins does (4, 191), that Kierkegaard's views are not individualistic and anti-social?

> And I don't want to know that feeling
> That people call love of people.
> I know only love of God.
> . . . .
> But for the dull and stupid race
> There can be no better love than hate.

These words of Ibsen's Brand could not agree more with the attitude inspired by Kierkegaard. (21, 3, 369 and 374) His religious fanaticism is but mystified egoism which tears the individual and society apart and reinforces the antagonism of the personal and the social. "Personality is a category of the spirit, of spiritual awakening, that is as hostile as possible to politics...." (cited from 51, 100)

Kierkegaard's theosophically mystified egocentrism leads to an antihumanist culmination.

> Humaneness is that feeble word
> That has become the watchword of the world!
> . . . .
> Soon, I suppose, on the prescription of the petty,
> Trivial souls, all people will become
> Apostles of humanity! But was Our Lord
> The Father himself humane towards his Son?
>   (21, 3, 392–393)

W. Andersen, a Danish interpreter of Kierkegaard, is fully justified in saying that this doctrine is "a radical break with humanism in the name of Christianity." (cited from 55, 129) What other description can be made of the position of a philosopher who demands that man "act not in the interests of man but for the glory of God," (*Diary*, 1852; cited from 6, 253) for the glory of "man's worst enemy"?

But was Kierkegaard's apoliticalness as apolitical as all that? His contempt for the human race is crystallized in contempt for the mass of people. What can be more expressive in that connection than his aphorism on the evangelical preachment of love for one's neighbor: "I have never read the moral in the Scriptures: Love the masses...." (6, 33, 105)? His diaries and books are strewn with contemptuous, hostile attacks on the masses of the people. Jolivet does not exaggerate when he speaks of Kierkegaard's "ochlophobia." (64, 74)

"I," Kierkegaard proclaims in his chief philosophical work, "did not intend to write a book that spoke in the name of millions, millions and billions." (6, 16, II, 332) Quite the contrary: the masses are his political target. The Biblical saying: the voice of the people is the voice of God, is not at all to his taste, and he remarks sarcastically that Cromwell contrived to make use of it in his political propaganda. (6, 16, II, 318) Oh no, he asserts, the mass is not at all the voice of truth: "There is a view of the world according to which where the mass is, there the truth is.... But there is another view of the world as well, according to which wherever the mass is, there untruth is." (6, 33, 99) This second world view is his world view, according to which the masses are the source of all the evil, all the chaos, that menaces us. (7, 259) For him, the most fearful form of tyranny is the tyranny of the masses. "Of all tyrannies, democracy is the most painful, the most soulless, the implacable downfall of everything great and exalted.... Democracy is the authentic image of Hades." (9, 245–247) The time has passed when war had to be made against tyrants; in the future, according to Kierkegaard, every true reformer will have to close ranks not against governments, not against reigning powers, but against the tyrannical desires of the masses. (7, 504 and 267) Kierkegaard's unsocialness is revealed as spiteful anti-populism.

Having said "A", Kierkegaard goes on to say "B": hostility to the people is followed immediately by militant hostility to democracy. For him, "democracy is the most tyrannical form of government." (6, 16, II, 334) The apolitical inhabitant of the ivory tower carries on an unceasing propaganda against any and all democratic movements and undertakings, even in their most limited liberal manifestations. Liberty, equality and fraternity are lying, false, deceptive slogans. "Long live human stupidity! That is what could be called freedom," reads an entry in 1848. (7, 298) There is only one form of freedom: inner freedom, freedom of the will, freedom to be oneself. But such freedom is incompatible with equality. Freedom excludes equality and reinforces inequality. In reality, there is only one equality: equality before God, before whom all of us are equal in our inequality. "To profess to solve the problem of equality among people while remaining in the earthly realm...means to condemn oneself to not being able to move a single step forward: that road is closed off forever...." (5, X2, A356)

Kierkegaard can not stomach popular participation in running the government, or even the parliamentary form of government. He rejects government based on voting, by counting "on buttons," (6, 33, 86) and limited by a legislative assembly. He stresses his love for the simple man, for the "lower class," (6, 33, 86) but inveighs against giving him freedom, a share in the power, setting up a democratic form of government. He is terrified by "the fourth estate, i.e. everybody." "Once the fourth estate comes into its own, it is obvious that secular power has become impossible." (6, 36, 205–207) For Kierkegaard, nothing is worse than democracy; it is "a tyrannical form of government," "one in which everyone wants to rule, and, in addition, force everyone to take part in government...." (6, 16, II, 334–335) The only proper governmental power is not from the people but from God. "Of all the forms of government, the monarchical is the best, absolute, hereditary monarchy." (6, 16, II, 334)

Kierkegaard "never took part in the political and social struggles that went on around him.... He had no faith in the value of sudden reforms and revolutionary uprisings. And he never believed in the kind of democracy that consists in letting the majority settle every question.... Clearly, therefore, he was a conservative," (retranslated from Russian) that is how Kierkegaard's politics are described by Hohlenberg, his biographer. (58, 277) Can that be called being apolitical? Was not his "apoliticalness" the reverse side of his political conservatism and opposition to democracy?

"Elementary scientific conscience will not allow us to deny Kierkegaard's extreme political conservatism" (27, 302), and the overwhelming majority of students, for all the variation in their evaluations of his views, agree that "he himself was as conservative as it is possible to be...." (42, 9) In Jaspers' words, "he did not want to have anything to do with the socialists, or the liberals, or any politicians and agitators who advanced programs for changing the social order." (60, 304) And could it have been otherwise? "He who rejects any intrusion into external activity as an abandonment of internal essence must of necessity sanction existing relations such as they are." (27, 302)

Kierkegaard does not try to make a secret of his political conservatism; he flaunts it. In his *Diary* we find an open admission that all his work "is a defense of what exists, the only thing that can be done without trampling on truth." (7, 523) He declares this publicly as well: "I was never in opposition and never took part in it, in their efforts to overthrow the government." (6, 33, 14–15) During the period of the liberal-reformist movements of the 1830s, he took a vigorous stand against them. His articles in the Copenhagen *Flygposten* leave no doubt as to that.

Kierkegaard was infuriated even more by the revolutionary ideas and movements that sprang up in various countries of Europe in 1830, and still more in 1848. He did not consider the defeat of the revolution as a catastrophe, but rather the fact that it happened. He saw nothing but brutality, violence, barbarism in the revolutionary uprisings against the brutality, violence and barbarism of the existing order. He was particularly dismayed that "at the same instant, at the same sound of the tocsin at which the bourgeoisie decided to take power, the fourth estate rose." (cited from 76, 271)

Only obscurantists like Brun, who contrasts Kierkegaard's Christianity to the atheistic humanism of Feuerbach, who greeted the revolution, can say that it is a great mistake to call Kierkegaard's political views counter-revolutionary and reactionary. (cf. 39, 36 and 41) But what would Brun say to these statements by Kierkegaard? "The evil of our time is not the existing state of affairs with its many defects; no, the evil of our time lies in this fierce inclination towards reforming lusts, to this playing with them...." (6, 27–29, 240) "Crushing princes and the Pope is not difficult as compared with the struggle against the masses, against the tyranny of equality, against the baseness of the absence of spirituality." (7, 343) And finally, what can be more explicit than this counter-revolutionary tirade: "When any rebellious nature enters into conflict with his times, he puts his bond to God up for sale, even if not for money"? (6, 16, I, 126)

Such is the political nature of the "apolitical" Kierkegaard. This is the political meaning that emerges from his contraposition of the eternal and the future. For the conservative, "being apolitical," calling for conservation of the existing order, is the most fitting of policies. "...The misfortune of our time," Kierkegaard tells us, "in politics, in religion and in everything else, is disobedience, that is what is inexcusable." (6, 35, 5) He ends his *Gospel of Suffering* with an apology for submissiveness. In the *Diary* he exclaims, with feeling: "What our age needs...is the martyr, he who, to teach people obedience, was himself faithful unto death...." (7, 287)

What Kierkegaard dreads most of all is the revolt of the masses. "The multitude is untruth" (6, 33, 89), he says flatly; it is impossible to rely on the masses, to achieve one's ends by means of the cooperation of the masses, to get them into motion. He declares against any kind of organization, association, cooperation of the masses of the people. On the contrary, everything possible must be done to split and divide the masses, to break them up into "individuals." Every man should struggle for himself, for his personal salvation. In contrast to Stirner's "I have wagered my all on myself and all the world belongs to me," Kierkegaard wagers his all on himself in his fanatical contempt for the world. The unity of the personal and the social is denied in both cases: in one as naked anarchical individualism, in the other as mystified egocentrism. As Löwith says, for all their antagonism Kierkegaard and Max Stirner "meet here as the antipodes to Marx" (76, 269), and, it should be added, to any progressive ideology in general.

In Kierkegaard the philosophical underpinning of these reactionary conclusions is his treatment of the problem of the "individual and society," which for him assumes the form of the problem: personality, society and deity – the particular, the general and the absolute.

In the *Concept of Dread* we find sound and sober judgments by Kierkegaard on the determinant influence of social life and historical development on the formation of the personality, and on the inseparable interconnection of the individual and the social. We find here such statements as that "the entire race participates in the individual, and the individual in the race," (6, 11–12, 25) that "no individual is indifferent to the history of the race, just as the race to each individual." (6, 11–12, 26) It is only with the forward movement of the human race, Kierkegaard continues, that the forward movement of the individual begins and historical development is carried on along with it. "Every individual," he writes, "has its principle in historical connection, and the natural consequences of this retain their significance now, as previously." (6, 11–12 73) In the section "The Influence of Historical Relations" we find the following statement on the formation of the personality: "In and of itself, the infant, and most children, is neither good nor bad; but it comes into a good society and becomes good, or into a bad society and becomes bad. Influences of the milieu! Influences of the milieu!" (6, 11–12, 77) There is nothing new or divergent from undisputed premises in these statements. But it is not they that determine the "climate" of Kierkegaard's world view. In fact, it is hard to see how they can be reconciled with his world view. For that view is shot through and through with denial of the unity and interdependence of the personal and the social, the individual and the socio-historical. For it requires, through and through, a divorce, a contraposition, a conflict between one and the other: either–or.

Against the Aristotelian definition of man as *zoon politikon* (a political animal) Kierkegaard advances as the basic, determinant distinction between man and animal, not his social nature but his individuality, his individual personality, ignoring the crucial fact that the formation of man as a person is an outgrowth or product of social, historical development. The metaphysical antithesis of individual and race does more than push into the background the Aristotelian principle as the necessary starting point for a correct understanding of the question: it pushes that principle quite out of the picture.

On this Kierkegaard says: "This is the problem, which in my opinion is one of the most important: how and to what extent society is determined by individuals and what the relationship is of the individual to society." (6, 16, I, 144) "And right *here* is where the battle must be fought," he says (7, 446), dashing into the fray.

For Kierkegaard the key problem is that of the individual and society, and solution of it is the link that is to bind together his ethical, political and religious views. Despite his professions of concreteness, he poses and resolves the problem in disregard of any and all concrete historical conditions, in a manner that is applicable to any society, to society in general. For him, being concrete means appertaining to the personality as "individual," related not to a particular society but to society outside of history as the anti-personal principle.

Kierkegaard's answer to the question of the relation of individual and society is: the person is primary, society secondary. "The individual," in his words, "is what is dialectically decisive, as being primary for the formation of the community...." (29, 69) The person is the axis around which everything human revolves. The "individual" is a category that "runs through time, history and society." (6, 33, 112) And the primacy of the personality is understood here as not only and not primarily genetically but (and this is the nub of the matter for Kierkegaard) also normatively, teleologically, axiologically. And it is in this primacy of the personality and its superiority to society that the distinctive feature of human existence consists. "Man is qualitatively distinguished from the other animal species... by the fact that the personality, the individual, is higher than the race." (6, 24–25, 122)

All history, according to Kierkegaard, is the history of the struggle between the personality and society, the individual and the race, between which there is an unceasing antagonism. The individual must rebel against the society that crushes it, overthrow the power of the race, gain freedom from the oppression of history. There is no historical possibility in Kierkegaard's field of vision for the development of the individual to correspond to the interests of society and for that development to be realized on the basis of the social activity of the individual. Kierkegaard starts with the postulate of inextricable antagonism and advances as the basic task "rising above the multitude." "The formation of subjectivity is the highest task facing a human being...." (6, 16, I, 149)

Inasmuch as society is nothing but a multipicity, an assemblage of, individuals, a "mass," a "public," the antagonism of the individual and the social takes the form of a conflict between the "unique" and the "mass." "If the multitude is the evil, the chaos threatening us, then safety lies only in one thing: to become isolated...." (6, 33, 64) And Kierkegaard calls: "...away from the public to the individual." (6, 33, 9) And since social activity and political struggle are public, the conclusion that follows inevitably is to refrain from social struggle, political reforms and historical transformations. "The false way lies directly before us," he wrote in 1849, "reform, trying to arouse the whole world, instead of arousing oneself...." (7, 396) "Personality is a category of the spirit, of spiritual development, and is as opposed as can be to politics." (6, 33, 115) But, as we have seen, this "denial" of politics is a form of political conservatism helping to retain the existing order of things.

Kierkegaard asserts that "certainly there is not another man living in the Kingdom of Denmark who has a feeling of individuality equal to mine" (7, 624); he is trying thereby to dissociate himself from egoism, to draw a dividing line between the "individual" and the "isolated." "For me each man unconditionally had infinite value," runs another entry in his *Diary*. (7, 624) But the absolute "individuality," the absence of any kind of common social interests uniting people, which Kierkegaard preaches, human disjunction: if these were actually realized, would they not lead inevitably to the *bellum omnium contra omnes*, to individualistic anarchy, to degrading social decadence? The heart of the matter is that a human being for whom all other people have infinite value cannot but be concerned with the social system which determines the fate of humanity. Otherwise the humanistic assurances remain empty phrases, those "good intentions" with which the road to hell is paved (not the hell in the beyond with which they try to frighten the godless, but the hell this side of the grave that still prevails today on most of the globe).

With such an approach to the relationship of the individual and society, unity, solidarity, any sort of social organization are condemned as standing in contradiction to "individuality" and confining it. Any social organizing, regardless of the goals it aims at, is identified with dehumanizing herding. The foremost consideration with respect to other people becomes the urge not to be like everybody else, to be unusual. Collectivity, with its "diabolical principle of leveling" (6, 17, 114) is contrasted to dissociation and disorganization. Kierkegaard depreciates the assimilation by each individual of the achievements of culture, his mastery of the historical accomplishments of civilization as depersonalizing factors, not as stimuli to progress aiding in the development of the individual and his ascent to a higher plane. "...Culture," in his words, "makes people insignificant; it perfects them as copies but deprives them of individuality..." (7, 592); it converts most people into "dulled *Egos*," (7, 627) and "trained monkeys." (9, II, 149)

Kierkegaard does not discuss humanity socially or humanistically, but anti-socially, individualistically. To the ideal of social harmony he contraposes monadic disconnection. The individual is not regarded dialectically as the boundary of the general, but antinomially as its alternative. Any harmony of thoughts, every collaboration, is represented as depersonalization in Kierkegaard's crooked mirror. It means that "they become people by virtue of aping others.... He is no different from others, therefore he is human." (7, 407) Nothing is more alien to Kierkegaard's views than the idea of the flowering of the personality as a function of collective creativity, participation in collective undertakings and achievements, spiritual mutual enrichment in the process of social working together and comradely mutual aid. The collective is inconceivable to him as accord of personalities, as unity of diversity in work, in research, in struggle for the general good. If, as we have seen, Kierkegaard's being "apolitical" with respect to the existing socio-political structure is nothing more than the most inert conservatism, the prophet of the cult of the "Unique" is implacably hostile to the socialist movement which arose in his days. "In the tempestuous period of the appearance of the new ferments of socialism and the first great workers' revolutions, he remained amazingly foreign to the problems created for society in the process of technological and political development." (49, 179) More than that: these problems were not only foreign to Kierkegaard, they terrified him; they evoked "fear and trembling" in him, although of a quite different nature than the fear due to original sin that he preached.

Kierkegaard's *Literary Communication*, which appeared in 1846, leaves no doubt as to his rejection and hatred of the young socialist workers' movement. Comparing the great and the small, Löwith calls it an "anticommunist manifesto." (76, 130) In it we can find: "We could not be further from believing that the idea of society, of the collective, will be the salvation of our times.... The principle of association (which can have the greatest of significances in relation to material interests) is not positive in our time but negative; it is a trap, an obscuration, a deception of the senses...." (6, 117, 113) The union of the multitude, strengthening individuals, weakens them morally. For Kierkegaard, socialism is not the liberation of the individual, opening up for him broad horizons of progress in every direction, but a trap to tie the individual down. "At the height of the European crisis in 1848 Kierkegaard shows himself a determined anti-revolutionary and anti-democrat." (51, 96) Entrusting his fears to the *Diary*, he writes: "Of all tyrannies, the tyranny of equality is the most dangerous.... Communism most of all leads to tyranny...." (8, 215) A man for whom the people, the masses of people were a bugbear and his own superiority an icon, could think in no other way.

Kierkegaard's intrinsically anti-humanist imagination paints the specter haunting Europe, the specter of communism, in lurid colors: "*Communism* says: this is how things should be in the world; there should no longer be any difference between one human being and another; riches, art, science, government, etc., etc., are evil; all people should be equal, like factory workers, like day laborers; they should be dressed alike and eat the same food, prepared in a huge pot, at the same sound of the bell, in the same amount, etc., etc." (6, 36, 208) Is not this crushing critique of communism fully worthy of the pen of the "deep thinker" and "keen judge" of human existence? To be fair, it is in no way inferior to the "anti-communist manifestoes" of our time.

Kierkegaard's political convictions were not based on any sort of serious study of the history of mankind or rational knowledge of the laws and motive forces of social development. He was guided exclusively by emotional anti-democratic motives, inseparable from his religious views. "Kierkegaard did not understand much about history," says S. Holm, the Copenhagen theologian, "either in the methodological or the cultural-sociological sense." (59, 6) We find the same accurate judgment in H. J. Blackham: Kierkegaard "lacked the historical interest and understanding for an adequate analysis of the social situation." (5, 21) "Can an historical starting point serve for eternal consciousness? How can such a starting point offer anything more than historical interest? Can eternal bliss be founded on historical knowledge?" Kierkegaard inquires rhetorically in the epigraph to his *Philosophical Sketches*. (6, 10) He does not only not aim at finding the objective laws of history but, with his discussion of the freedom of the will and the secondary nature of the social as compared with the individual, he demands abandonment of historical objectivity, which he regards as totally impermissible. "While for Kierkegaard," H. Rademacher remarks correctly in this connection, "it was already un-Christian, in considering nature, to lose oneself in approaching it as a world of objects having a reality of its own, it would be consciously un-Christian and heathen to take history as well as one's object." (88, 116) Philosophical fideism does not admit of scientific objectivity in general, nor of a scientific conception of history in particular. Between them lies an impassable chasm. The sphere of existence, the arena of human action, is not subject to objective law and is inaccessible to scientific knowledge. And all of this was written in the very years when the solidly scientific materialist conception of history was taking final form. Kierkegaard, to be sure, knew nothing of the theoretical results of the founders of Marxism, not of the revolutionary practice they founded on those results. One can easily imagine the anger and hostility he would have felt if he had come to know what he would have regarded as their "monstrous," "diabolical" doctrine. Neo-Thomist J. Collins, comparing the criticisms made of Hegel's theory of the state by Kierkegaard and Marx, observes that two Marxist theses would have been unacceptable to Kierkegaard: first, the assertion that "the welfare of the social economy is an absolute consideration," and secondly that the state "must meanwhile be used as an instrument for securing the triumph of the classless society." (41, 186) Apart from the fact that for the founders of scientific communism economic prosperity was not at all the final aim of the revolutionary transformation of the world but only a necessary means and indispensable condition for perfecting human being and consciousness, Collins could hardly manage to find even a *single* thesis of the Marxist doctrine of the origin, essence, forms and functions of the state that would have been *acceptable* to Kierkegaard. Their views were simply incommensurable.

As a counterweight to the unity and political organization of the most advanced people in the struggle for the vital interests of the masses of the people, who call for radical transformation of the existing order. Kierkegaard called for the union of the isolated individual with God. "I am fighting for eternity, concerned over the salvation of my soul." (6, 34, 305) In Christian dogma "salvation" is individualistic, otherworldly, irrationalist. It does not demand either social struggle or the unity of people holding the same views; it is not directed towards worldly welfare; it does not stand in need of any theoretical foundation. Human dignity is not defined by services to society nor by contributions to the development of material and spiritual culture nor by socially significant achievements, but by renunciation of everything mortal and historical, by being able to "complicate life and increase the burden" (7, 366), in atonement for sin and in the desire for eternal bliss. "For the greatness of man," Kierkegaard says, "depends solely and exclusively on the energy of his own relationship to God.... He is truly great not in the moment of brilliant outward display...but in *that* moment when he, thanks to himself and in his own presence, plunges into the depths of the consciousness of his sinfulness." (6, 11–12, 113) The course of religious ethics does not lie in the self-assertion of the individual in his unity with the social, but in separation from the general in the name of unity with the absolute, the divine. "The individual is higher than the universal, the individual...determines his relationship to the general through his relationship to the absolute, and not his relationship to the absolute through his relationship to the general." (6, 4, 76)

Such is the political conjugate of Kierkegaardian fideism. Mystical illusion covers social actuality with an impenetrable cloud. It would be hard to find a clearer illustration of the words of Lenin: "The idea of God has *always* dulled and blunted 'social feelings,' replacing what is living by what is dead; it is *always* the idea of slavery (the worst, irreparable slavery). The idea of God never 'linked the individual with society,' but always *bound* the oppressed *classes* by faith in the *divinity* of the oppressors." (3, 48, 232) These words could have been written directly against Kierkegaard, whose fideism goes over directly into a political conservatism which is indifferent to the real fate of social being, which determines human existence.

The last year of Kierkegaard's life was the year of his mutiny, revolt, insurrection. By his very nature he had always been restless, unbalanced, high-strung, easily ruffled. Easily ruffled, but not rebellious. And now this inveterate political conservative revolted, disturbing the peace, raising a storm "in this prostituted capital city of Philistinism, my cherished Copenhagen." (7, 343) The immediate occasion for the revolt was the death in 1854 of the head of the Danish Protestant church, Bishop Münster, the friend and spiritual mentor of Kierkegaard's father. While Münster was alive, Kierkegaard restrained himself but when his successor, Bishop Martensen, made a eulogy of his predecessor as a "witness to Christ," Kierkegaard rebelled and opened fire. He alone, the "individual," revolted against the most powerful spiritual force of his time who was unrivaled master of the minds and hearts of his fellow-citizens; he rose up against the established church. "In a series of articles in this newspaper (the *Fatherland* - B.B.) I now opened a vigorous fire, to speak in military language, against official Christianity and hence against the clergy in our country." (6, 34, 64) In half a year twenty-one militant anti-clerical articles by Kierkegaard were printed in the paper, and from May 24, 1855 a newspaper of his own began publication, financed with the last money left from his father's inheritance, the *Moment*, entirely devoted to the campaign he had begun in the *Fatherland*.

Münster with all his activity, incorporated in the Danish Protestant clerical system, was not only the occasion but the ground for Kierkegaard's vigorous attack on the existing Christian church. In his merciless critique of Münster and his affairs he condemned the entire basis, the entire structure, the entire practice of church life both in the Danish kingdom and beyond its borders. Kierkegaard referred to Martensen himself, so highly praised and exalted by the clericals, as a "poisonous plant," and to his activity as the spreading of "monstrous corruption." (6, 35, 269) But this criticism went far beyond the local framework; it was not confined to criticizing Münster as a local phenomenon.

How could the bitter enemy of revolution and maligner of reforms, the advocate of the absolute monarchy, thrice honored with a personal audience with Christian VIII, how could he rebel against the main ideological support of the existing system, against the religious establishment, against the age-old traditions of the Christian Church? How could this zealot of faith, this enthusiast of Christianity, engage in mutiny against the ministers of religion, the chanters of the kingdom of God?

He mutinied precisely because he was a fanatic for Christianity, a "knight of faith." He mutinied against the church in the name of Christianity, convinced that "what is preached in the world under the title of Christianity is not, strictly speaking, Christianity...." (6, 33, 144)

"Oh, Luther put forward ninety-five theses.... Yet there is only one thesis...." (6, 34, 42) What the priests give out as Christianity is not the Christianity of the New Testament, not the authentic faith of Christ, but "a caricature of real Christianity or an incredible aggregate of errors and illusions etc...." (6, 33, 76), "a monstrous deception of the feelings," a falsification and demoralization of religious faith by "the so-called church." (7, 620) What does this "Christendom" have in common with "Christianity"? "Christendom is rotten Christianity; and the so-called Christian world is nothing but the abandonment of Christianity." (6, 34, 44) From generation to generation Christianity kept degenerating and in the end degenerated to such a point that it was transformed into its opposite: the society that is called "Christian" has become "the society of un-Christians." (6, 34, 239)

Kierkegaard's critique of the established church is merciless. He bitterly mocks the ritual and service of the church. The baptism rite is a mockery of Christianity, for the infant cannot yet be a Christian. Confirmation and ordination are a "Christian comedy performance, if not something worse." (6, 34, 239) The marriage ceremonies are a mockery of Christianity; the true Christian should not get married at all (and Kierkegaard is not in the least alarmed that the ideal of celibacy would sentence the human race to extinction). Church sermons are mere hypocrisy. "The difference between a church and a theater is that the theater honorably and truthfully recognizes what it is; but the church, unlike the theater, mendaciously tries by all means to hide what it is." (6, 34, 218) Kierkegaard repeats that all the rites of the church, all the church services, "take God for a fool." (6, 34, 29)

Pastors, priests, bishops? That is plainly and simply nothing more than an occupation, "a way of making a living, like any other way of making a living in society...." (6, 34, 31) Kierkegaard calls for the liquidation of the pastorate for the sake of the triumph of Christianity. Pastors are not only hypocrites but extortioners, careerists, profiting by their hypocrisy. "Looking at a pastor, you can not help coming to the conclusion that Christianity is not yet truth, but truth is what is profitable." (6, 34, 316) The ninth number of the *Moment*, the last to appear in Kierkegaard's lifetime, has an article "That Pastors Are Cannibals, and in the Vilest Way." "A cannibal," Kierkegaard explains, "is a savage; a 'pastor' is a learned, educated man, which makes his baseness all the more disgraceful. His cannibalism is well thought out, shrewdly planned...." (6, 34, 313) When you see a priest, Kierkegaard advises, run from him (6, 34, 335), from that "symbol of folly enveloped in a long surplice." (6, 34, 184)

Not surprisingly, these fierce attacks on the church evoked not only the furious rage of the clerics of Copenhagen but also general disapproval on the part of the residents of the "prostituted capital city of Philistinism." Christianity was not Hegelianism, which had penetrated into the minds of a very thin stratum of the cream of Danish intellectuals, but a tradition of every "decent person," one which was indisputable, unalterable, inculcated from earliest childhood. The *Moment* called forth a storm of indignation and scorn for the recreant who had outraged the inveterate feelings of the faithful, all the baptized god-fearing parishioners, all the flock of Münster and Martensen. And a theologian at that, a master of theology! A monstrous offspring who had dared to say publicly: "I had rather play cards, get drunk, lead a depraved life, than take part in an activity that takes God for a fool." (6, 34, 27)

Kierkegaard's criticism of the established church, for all its harshness and militancy, was not in any way an anti-religious critique in general or a critique of the Christian religion in particular. It was a critique of Christian actuality as it *is* from the point of view of what it *ought* to be strictly following the precepts of the Gospel. When a Catholic commentator on Kierkegaard asks the rhetorical question: "Was Kierkegaard really a Christian?", (64, 237) he overlooks the fact that the Danish thinker was not an apostate but a zealot for Christian ideals, one who denounced the formalism, hypocrisy and sanctimony of both the clerics and the devout laity, who professed to be observers of the Christian faith while at the same time destroying, corrupting and betraying it at every step, by their entire way of life. In the words of Jaspers, "he saw in his epoch, with a radicalism hardly matched by anyone else at the time, the decay of the Western European substance. Insofar as the 'real' had become a lie, he rose up against the real, regarding himself as appointed by God to become the victim of the age, and offering himself as the victim." (60, 315–317) He rose up in protest against the church's diminution and softening of rigorous Christianity, against the ease with which it adapted to worldly requirements and demands. His fundamental charge was: "What exists is an open betrayal of the Christianity of the New Testament...it is an attempt to take God for a fool." (6, 34, 26)

In reading Kierkegaard's denunciations of the men of the church and the church practices, which are just as sharp as the denunciations by Holbach and Feuerbach, we should not forget the basic contrast of the motive forces and directions of the two parties. Kierkegaard's Philippics are not aimed at Christian beliefs. Protestantism, rejecting the canonization of saints and martyrs, canonized Everyman, the Philistine. (cf. 7, 354)* The existing church does not fight for their conversion into Christians but overshadows them with the sign of the cross and blesses them such as they are. The men of the church possess Christianity; Christianity does not possess them. There, in Kierkegaard's opinion, is the root of the evil.

How can Kierkegaard's political conservatism jibe with his religious dissidence? Actually, they not only jibed but coexisted, complementing one another. It was no accident that Kierkegaard's "only thesis:" "There is no longer a Christianity!", "This is not Christianity!", to the disclosure and propaganda of which he devoted all his literary activity in the *Fatherland* and the *Moment*, was proclaimed in the year of 1848. In the year of the revolutionary movement that rocked Europe, Kierkegaard called for the restoration of primitive Christianity. It was an isolated cry, the voice of one crying in the wilderness, an unrealizable Christian Utopia. The "leap" that Kierkegaard called on every "individual" to make in the "moment" of decision was in the direction of the distant past, the irrevocable age of early Christianity. His mutinous "innovation" called for a resurrection of the form of consciousness of the era of the decadence of ancient slaveholding society. It was "innovation" turned towards the past, towards antique traditions long since discarded in the course of the history of Christianity and pulverized in the mills of feudalism and capitalism. The cause for which Kierkegaard fought to his dying hour with ever-increasing passion was a reactionary Utopia: "Back to Christianity!" (6, 33, 74) "Roll back 1800 years as if they had never existed." (cited from 88, 90)

The Utopia of a return to primitive Christianity was not new by any

---

* Jolivet cites these statements of Kierkegaard's and interprets them as a criticism of Protestantism, neglecting the fact that Kierkegaard's accusations of sanctimony, ritualism and corruption in the church hierarchy apply to an even greater degree to the Catholic church.

means. But whereas it had had a progressive, genuinely democratic character in the Moravian Brethren and the Hussites, expressing, in a religious vestment, the innermost aspirations of the oppressed masses, that same Utopia in Kierkegaard, in the years of the bourgeois-democratic revolution, took on an entirely different resonance, losing its democratic and progressive character. In Kierkegaard's eyes the leveling communism of the Hussites would appear like the same hated attack on the rights and freedom of the "individual" that he fiercely rejected as the inevitable concomitant of any democratic organization.

What has been said as to the reactionary nature of Kierkegaard's Utopia is not at all contradicted by the progressive-sounding demand he made for the separation of church and state, directed against thousands of pastors transformed into thousands of functionaries receiving thousands of stipends. But Kierkegaard was not aroused to make this demand by concern for freedom of conscience, for religious tolerance, nor by opposition to the sanctification of the power of the state, but by the same old fanatical eschewal of worldly, social interests, the same old preachment of his – "to die to the world." The political conservatism and the fanatical Christian Utopianism not only did not contradict one another: they reinforced one another. Rendering unto God what is God's, Kierkegaard rendered unto Caesar what is Caesar's. In him separation of church and state coincided with the unchangeability and untouchability of the existing socio-political structure. Whereas for the young Hegel the separation of church and state was one of the conditions for successful struggle against religious orthodoxy,* for Kierkegaard it was one of the conditions for the restoration of orthodox Christianity.

Objectively, the political sense of the entire anti-church revolt by Kierkegaard consisted in a *switch* from political interests to purely religious absorption in self, in a diversion from social reforms and social struggle to church reforms aimed at withdrawal from genuine vital interests. Considered on the political plane, Kierkegaard's Christian Utopia is pathetic religious escapism, a fanatical call for evasion from the news of the day into the mystical distance of religious illusions. In Kierkegaard's own words, "the religious is the reproduction, in the trappings of eternity, of the fairest dreams of politics." (6, 33, 97) Only let everything on earth remain as it is. The best is not of this earth. "Essentially, the church should represent the future, and the state, on the contrary, that which is not transient. That it is why it is so dangerous

---

* "Religion and politics are for the same thing," Hegel wrote to his then friend Schelling in 1795. "The former taught what despotism had in view: contempt for the human race...." (cited from 25, 1, 33)

for the state and the church to grow together like Siamese twins, and become identical." (8, 3, 165)

Kierkegaard's Christian Utopia is an ideal, both unrealizable and reactionary, of the anarchic coexistence of "individuals" immersed in themselves, each suffering in his own way in expiation of the sin of Adam and Eve, striving in narcotic trembling towards the beyond, the incorporeal, eternal bliss in the radiant heavenly kingdom. Blessed is he who believes despite reason, in the teeth of the elements!

CHAPTER VIII

THE SECOND COMING

Kierkegaard remained true to himself. He refused to receive the sacraments from the hands of a priest. He did not want to obtain a passport into the kingdom of heaven from the rotten church. Censured by the clericals, the "Danish Socrates" drank to the dregs the hemlock of public indignation. His fellow-citizens rested easier: the troublemaker, the disturber of the peace, was no more. But it seemed as though his historical existence had come to an end along with his physical existence. It was a long time until the tenth number of the *Moment* appeared. A quarter of a century elapsed before the publication of his *Diary*. His works and edifying orations had no influence whatever on his compatriots. And outside Denmark he remained totally unknown. The founders of Marxism, who followed so keenly the ideology hostile to the revolutionary socialist movement, had no knowledge of his existence or his works. There was every reason why his doctrine remained unknown to their great successor as well: Kierkegaard left no followers in Denmark, let alone outside it. The history of philosophy consigned him to oblivion. The extensive and detailed biographical dictionary of philosophers compiled by L. Noack (1879) does not even mention Kierkegaard.

But, as the saying goes, books have their fates. While the first translations into German of works by Kierkegaard, *A Self-Criticism of the Present Time Is Needed* (1869), *Education for Christianity* (1878), remained unnoticed, the situation changed at the beginning of this century. Protestant theologians were the first to "discover" Kierkegaard. Schrempf, Hecker, Brunner, Barth, Bultman adopted his fideism for their arsenal. In 1909 the first German edition of Kierkegaard's collected works began to appear. The German language opened the way to him for the philosophers of Western Europe. But the true resurrection of Kierkegaard from the dead took place in the years of World War I. "It was only with the first world war," Jaspers testifies, "that the Danish thinker and poet who died in 1855 became really known in Germany and the foundation of modern philosophizing." (60, 498) "And it was no accident," observes A. Paulsen in this connection, "that it was only after the first world war that he was, in fact, first discovered, and in Germany, and this discovery, it must be said, led to a spiritual transformation in the postwar period."

(85, 440) Yes, this "discovery" was not accidental. Nor was it an accident that in the postwar period Kierkegaard became a regular philosophical idol of the German, and then the French, idealists. "Philosophy without Kierkegaard seems to me to be impossible in our times," declared Jaspers. (62, 2, XX) Interest in him grew to such a point that some philosophers, theologians and poets (for example, Rainer Maria Rilke) embarked on the study of Danish in order to come to grips with Kierkegaard's ideas. Copenhagen became the Bethlehem of existentialism.

From the first quarter of our century on, what has been called the Kierkegaard renaissance began. In the words of one of his most influential followers, Kierkegaard was "one of those roosters whose voice as it were announces to us, far and near, the actual approach of a new day." (33, 98) The prophecy of Kierkegaard himself was fulfilled; he had written in his *Diary:* "When the storm begins to hover over some generation, then individuals like me will appear." (cited from 85, 291)

During the second quarter of the twentieth century, when imperialism was leading up to the second world war, the influence of Kierkegaardianism on bourgeois ideology not only did not slacken but was reinforced and extended its field of attraction. To Protestant theologians were added some Catholic philosophers (such as Gabriel Marcel), whose number kept growing. Kierkegaard's doctrine also found its way into some transatlantic circles (originally through the Protestant theologians Tillich, Niebuhr and Lowrie.) "His name was practically unknown in our country (the U.S.A. – B.B.)," Collins says, "until the late nineteen-twenties, even though a Kierkegaard renaissance had been in full swing in Europe during the previous quarter of a century." (41, vii) Finally, Kierkegaard's voice was heard across the other ocean: a translation of his complete works was published in Japan in 1950. The center of the international "Kierkegaard Society" was founded in Copenhagen in 1948 and publishes a special journal, *Kierkegaardiana*. Translations of Kierkegaard's works and literature concerning him increases year by year. During the five years 1961–1965 alone over three hundred works on his life and doctrine appeared in various countries. Special national and international symposia are devoted to him.

Actually, it is impossible to speak of a "renaissance" of Kierkegaard's philosophy since it never had a "first youth." "His age did not understand him." (67, 263) L. Krieger is right when he says that "the vitality of his ideas belongs more to the twentieth century than to his own." (72, 241) (retrans. from Russian)

Our interest in Kierkegaard is not due to mere curiosity. It is conditioned and justified by the indisputable fact that the apparently stillborn doctrine came to life, acquired great influence in the spiritual life of today's bourgeois world, became a real ideological force reaching far beyond the framework of academic circles and percolating from philosophy and theology into *belles lettres*, poetry, drama, while making an impression on certain political theories. To be sure, it is impossible to agree with the statement that "while Kierkegaard meant nothing in the spiritual history of the nineteenth century, on the other hand the entire problematic of our century was concentrated and condensed in his work, as in a nucleus." (42, 7) And it is a manifest exaggeration to hold that "today, more than a hundred years after his death...he is one of the most influential, if not the most influential, philosophers of our time." (90, 55) Nonetheless, the weight of Kierkegaardianism in the idealist camp of contemporary philosophy is very significant, and his influence cannot be ignored or passed over. It cannot be denied that to a certain extent "Kierkegaard's production today is a living and active spiritual force," (56, 156) that "at the present time the world is interested in Kierkegaard as never before" and that "the seeds he planted a century ago are now beginning to sprout." (58, 294) (retrans. from Russian)

What is the secret of Kierkegaard's "second coming"? In general, there have been many cases in history of thinkers, discoverers, precursors who were not recognized, understood or appreciated in their lifetimes. Many scientific discoveries and technological inventions were made long before productive forces reached a level at which the forgotten early conjectures and surmises were realized. But there have also been many cases in history of errors, illusions and impostures that for many years, sometimes centuries, after their fabrication were brakes on social progress, spiritual weapons of reactionary forces. Mankind has experienced, and is now experiencing, many such restorations. One well-known case is neoscholasticism. And another example is the spiritual heritage of Sören Kierkegaard. His morbid psyche, injured consciousness and wavering thought gave birth in remote Copenhagen to ideas, feelings and impulses that suited to the tastes and spirit of the people of another century, which responded to the moods and desires of people living not only in other countries but under different social conditions, the conditions of the general crisis of the capitalist system.

Today's apologists for and admirers of Kierkegaard, losing all sense of proportion, exalt him as a thinker "whose religious philosophy ...has the same sort of significance for the future as Aristotle's *Organon* had in the history of logic" (34, 69); as a philosopher "who belongs forever to all mankind as solidly as Plato and Aristotle, Spinoza, Hume, Kant and Hegel" (D. F. Swenson in his preface to the English translation of Geismar, 45, XVII.) (retrans. from Russian) The standard-bearers of existentialism speak of the "Copernican revolution" in philosophy carried out in Copenhagen in the first half of last century, which put an end to the "Ptolemaic" systems of classical German philosophy* and laid the foundation of a new era in the history of philosophy, an entirely new kind of philosophizing....

Neither the so-called dialectical theology nor existentialism, whose basic theoretical source is the doctrine of Kierkegaard, form a single homogeneous trend, and none of their variants constitutes the unqualified, orthodox reproduction of that doctrine. "We are confronted with several rival interpretations of Kierkegaard's viewpoint, each one representing itself as the authentic version." (41, 179) Some of the philosophical trends deriving from his principles do not even consider themselves as his successors and differ from his conclusions in important respects. The Protestant theologians in Germany who first went over to him ended up by departing from him: Hecker became a Catholic and Schrempf abandoned religion. The proponents of "dialectical theology" too do not merely repeat Kierkegaard but revise him (perhaps the closest to Kierkegaard's doctrine is the theology of Hohgarten). As for the existentialist philosophers, it is characteristic of them that they make every effort to stress, not the Kierkegaardian tradition common to all of them but rather their differences with him. Some leaders of existentialism even refuse to have their doctrines so designated. Jaspers, characterizing Kierkegaard, said: "...A great error, developed on a broad scale, becomes so evident once and for all that it is not repeated any more. Insofar as he did this, later (philosophers) can learn from him what they now must clearly avoid." (60, 276) This thought is perfectly correct, but it is not exemplified in any of the existentialists, including Jaspers himself.

But for all their diversity and polemics with one another, and for all their varying attitudes towards religion [some are Protestants, others Catholics (Gabriel Marcel), others Judaists (Martin Buber), still others atheists (Sartre), while some (Heidegger) take an evasive position**], the theories of all of them are permeated deeply by a current that flows directly from Kierkegaard as its source – irrationalism. "The philosophy of our days has split into purely scientific study with limited objectives, and a philosophy of life, devoted to the key problems of existence and therefore making no claims of being scientific in the strict sense of the

---

* Rather, the opposite: does not the Kierkegaardian Universe revolve around man, and the individual at that? Is it not egocentric and not sociocentric, and "of the moment" at that, not historical as in Kant–Laplace?

** Existentialists are no less discordant on political questions: from Heidegger's groveling before Hitlerism, through Jaspers's half-way position – anti-fascist and anti-communist at the same time – to ultra-left rebelliousness.

word.... Kierkegaard is the source for all existentialist thinkers." (89, 158) By excluding from the field of vision of philosophy everything that does not relate to "existence" in the specific anthropological sense given the term by existentialists, the representatives of the philosophy of existence thereby reject the application of scientific, rational methods of knowledge in philosophy, and of logical, pseudo-rational methods and demonstrations in theology. This applies equally to atheistic existentialism and to "dialectical theology." Both these schools, albeit in different ways, parade a "dialectics" which, as in Kierkegaard himself, serve as a peculiar disguise for irrationalism, a "mythical guiding star," to use Adorno's apt expression. (27, 107)

In this respect, incidentally, the existentialists had forerunners who apparently had nothing in common with the existentialists. I have in mind the neo-Hegelian school, which in this regard is not far from the Kierkegaardian anti-Hegelianism. In the turn of contemporary idealist philosophy towards irrationalism, "extremes" meet. For all the contrariety of their attitudes towards the philosophical heritage of Hegel, their similarity is that both groups essentially deny the Hegelian dialectic: one openly denies the dialectic as logic, while the other does so covertly, by way of transforming the dialectical logic into its own opposite, which sanctions the right to live of irrationalist alogism.

It is curious that some interpreters of Kierkegaard try, in the face of Kierkegaard himself, not to contrapose him to Hegel but to bring them together on the basis of an alleged Hegelian "irrationalism." Thus, for example, I. Bogen flatly declares: "...Hegel was no less an irrationalist or arationalist than Kierkegaard was a 'rationalist" in exactly the same sense as Hegel was." (38, 374; retrans. from the Russian) All the difference between them, in Bogen's opinion, is "merely" that "in Kierkegaard's system (!) the synthesis is performed by God...while the Hegelian synthesis is performed by reason and is conceivable only in the logic of reason. It is just on *this* point that the two systems diverge." (38, 385; retrans. from the Russian) Equally "convincing" are Collins' arguments to the effect that Kierkegaard's point of view is "not antilogical and irrational." He "merely" insists on the difference between logic and metaphysics and asserts that "the act of existence is beyond the limits of what is attainable by any philosophical discipline," that "logic is brought up short by real existence and the existential determinants of real movement, and is indifferent to them." (40, 121–122; retrans. from the Russian) That sort of "rationalism" will not trouble either neo-Hegelians nor Kierkegaardians, nor will "dialectics", presented in such a way. In the years of the tremendous flowering of scientific thought and up-soaring of logical science, in the years of colossal scientific achievements, opening up horizons beyond the wildest fancy, bourgeois ideology resorts to an anti-scientific, alogical philosophy. And even Catholic philosophers, who hitherto have imitated the strict "logicality" of their creed, are now, in our days, when "even...churches...must be air-conditioned today," (87, 95) increasingly drawn to the existentialism that was condemned in the papal encyclical *Humani generis* (1950).* This phenomenon, like all real contradiction in actuality, is quite normal.

The socio-psychological basis which explains the spread of existentialism is the accordance of Kierkegaardian irrationalism with the spiritual climate of the age of the sunset of capitalism, "the twilight of the West," as Heidegger puts it. "The human condition may well be tragic in the latter half of the twentieth century," writes personalist A. Lessing in his article, "Hegel and Existentialism: On Unhappiness." We cannot hide the fact that in spite of the positive success of science, technology, democratic opportunity, and the rising standard of living, a great deal of individual life remains under the spell of despair, sadness, and, above all, incompleteness. It is to this condition that the philosophy of existence addresses itself." (73, 76 and 61–62) The "tragic dialectics" of S. Mark, the neo-Hegelian, already drives philosophy in that direction. Existentialism, in all its manifestations, constitutes a philosophical expression of the deep spiritual crisis inevitable in the epoch of the degeneration of capitalist society. If Protestant theology, under the influence of Kierkegaardianism, is known as "the theology of crisis," neo-Kierkegaardianism as a whole is nothing but the philosophy of crisis. It is "an expression of the situation in which the crumbling structure finds itself today, a philosophy of fragmentation, of the absence of points of support due to the hidden problems of lack of confidence in people's own security... a situation of despair.... It is an adequate expression, the heart-rending cry of man in a critical condition." (53, 396–398) "In Kierkegaard's sickness," says Thompson, "we find the universally human." (93, 45; retrans. from the Russian) A philosophy of dread, of alarm, of despair, of abandonment, of doom, of death – these are usual descriptions of existentialism by its own promulgators, who substitute "existentials" and "boundary situations" for traditional philosophical categories and make of them the only object of their distressing reflections.

Kierkegaard once compared himself to a man living in a garret which is about to tumble down, and he knows it. That is why people living in a society doomed to collapse recognized themselves in his philosophy, people who "had lost the ground under their feet." (82, 274) Uneasiness,

---

* After this encyclical by Pius XII, Gabriel Marcel, the French Catholic existentialist, called his doctrine "neo-Socraticism," quite in the spirit of Kierkegaard.

perplexity, profound pessimism, which they try vainly to overcome by empty illusions that fade away like smoke, create a psychological atmosphere highly favorable to the penetration of people's consciousness by existentialism. "The world of the XX century, enveloped in the convulsions of wars and revolutions, in economic and social crises, can no longer recognize itself in rose-colored philosophical productions. But it does recognize itself in Kierkegaard's tragic meditations and his active pessimism." (51, 117) How can one speak of "rational activity" in capitalist society in an age of imperialist wars, fascist barbarity, nuclear menace hanging over humanity? On what rationalism, what logic, what normality can bourgeois ideology be founded, when they not only forecast but bear within them the ruin of all the traditions and institutions of the bourgeoisie, its entire structure and way of life, of everything without which bourgois *existence is unthinkable.* The personal pathopsychology of the "individual" has become the mouthpiece of the mindless world writhing in its spiritual convulsions. "Kierkegaard, perhaps, was sick, but so are we all," Gusdorf frankly avows. (51, 107) "The great disease of our age," was the diagnosis of the Harvard University Health Services, "is aimlessness, boredom and lack of meaning and purpose in living." (cited from 26, 51)

The judgments and evaluations we have adduced are not by outsiders or strangers hostile to the capitalist world, but are testimony from within that world, confessions of people about the world in which they live, a world whose cares, interests, dispositions and agitations are their interests and dispositions. We have cited frank statements of the usual, "natural," "normal" experiences of a man living, existing in a distorted, diseased world, where "to exist" means a constant struggle to get through the barbed wire of *insoluble* contradictions.

What is there to be surprised at if existentialism is the philosophy most in keeping with this milieu? What is surprising in the fact that in that world Kierkegaard appears in the role of a far-sighted prophet? "For is not the nature of such a sick epoch as ours such, that a thinker deeply immersed in his internal world, pressed, neurotic, may finally find the way to people's hearts and – startling contradiction! – inspire renewed life into a weary world?" These are the words with which Marguerite Grimault concludes her study on "Kierkegaard's melancholy." (50, 203) Yes, he reflects that world; he gives a consciousness of the meaninglessness of such an existence, a philosophical expression to decadence; but "renewal"? Existentialism is a spiritual outcome of that same world that condemns people to meaningless existence. The existentialist, aware of this, disavowing that world, condemning it, does not break with it; he does not rise up against it, does not fight for its overthrow, its reconstruction, for the building of another, a new world. Like Sisyphus in Albert Camus, he has coalesced with his sufferings, has come to love them, cannot and will not part with them: that is *his* world, *his* life, *his* suffering, to which he is irreparably accustomed.

Kierkegaardianism is the clearest and most typical form of the pandemia of irrationalism raging in contemporary idealist philosophy; for that philosophy reason is an outworn method of thinking, and scientific understanding of the world is reckoned as an archaic survival.

The conviction that rational knowledge is powerless, bankrupt, worthless, leads human thought into a blind alley. Irrationalism in general, and existentialism in particular, bar the way to the unlimited progress of human thought and allow only two alternatives: either fideism or absolute skepticism, the "philosophy of the absurd"; either blind faith or disbelief in everything; either the cult of illusion or nihilism.

BIBLIOGRAPHY

1. Marx, K. and Engels, F. *Iz rannikh proizvedenii* (From the Early Works). Moscow, 1956.
2. Marx, K. and Engels, F. *Sochineniya* (Works). 2nd ed.
3. Lenin, V. I. *Polnoe sobranie sochinenii* (Complete Works). Moscow, 1958–1966. 5th ed.
4. Kierkegaard, S. *Samlede Vaerker*. Köpenhagen, 1920–1936.
5. Kierkegaard, S. *Papirer*. Köpenhagen, 1909–1948.
6. Kierkegaard, S. *Gesammelte Werke*. Düsseldorf, 1951–1962.
7. Kierkegaard, S. *Tagebücher*. München, 1953.
8. Kierkegaard, S. *Journal*. Paris, 1941–1957.
9. Kierkegaard, S. *Die Tagebücher*. Düsseldorf, 1962–1963.
10. Kierkegaard, S. *Naslazhdenie u dolg* (Enjoyment and Duty). St. Petersburg, 1904.
11. Kierkegaard, S. *Neschastneishii* (The Most Unhappy Man), St. Petersburg, 1908.
12. Kierkegaard, S. *Aforizmy estetiki* (Esthetic Aphorisms). "Vestnik Europý", 1886, vol. III.
13. Andersen, H. C. *Izbrannye sochineniya* (Selected Works), vol. I, Moscow, 1969.
14. Bakunin, M. I. *Sobranie sochinenii i pisem* (Collected Works and Letters), vol. III, Moscow, 1935.
15. Gaidenko, P. P. *Tragediya estetizma* (The Tragedy of Estheticism), Moscow, 1970.
16. Hegel, G. W. F. *Sochineniya* (Works), Moscow, 1929–1968.
17. Hegel, G. W. F. *Nauka logiki* (Science of Logic), Moscow, 1970.
18. Heine, H. *Sobranie sochinenii* (Collected Works), vol. VI, Leningrad, 1958.
19. Hertzen, A. I. *Izbrannye proisvedeniya* (Selected Works), Minsk, 1954.
20. Hertzen, A. I. *Byloe i dumy* (Memoirs), Moscow, 1970.
21. Ibsen, H. *Sochineniya* (Works), vol. III, Moscow, 1904.
22. Kant, I. *Sochineniya* (Works), Moscow, 1963–1966.
23. Kant, I. *Religiya v predelakh tol'ko razuma* (Religion within the Limits of Reason Alone), St. Petersburg, 1908.
24. Feuerbach, L. *Izbrannye filosofskie proizbedeniya* (Selected Philosophical Works), Moscow, 1955.
25. Fischer, K. *Istoriya novoi filosofii* (History of Modern Philosophy), vol. VII, St. Petersburg, 1905.
26. Adams, E. M. "What, if anything, can we expect from philosophy today?" *The Personalist* (Los Angeles), 1968, vol. 49, # 1.
27. Adorno, Th. W. *Kierkegaard: Konstruktion des Ästhetischen*, Frankfurt a. M., 1966.
28. Adorno, Th. W. *Negative Dialektik*, Frankfurt a. M., 1966.
29. Anz, W. *Kierkegaard und der deutsche Idealismus*, Tübingen, 1956.
30. Anz, W. "Zum Sokratverständnis Kierkegaards", *Orbis Litterarum*, Kopenhagen, 1963, vol. XVIII, # 1–2.
31. Arendt, H. "Marx, Kierkegaard und Nietzsche", *Preuves* (Paris), 1962, # 133.
32. Barth, H. "Die negative und die positive Philosophie", *Studia philosophica* (Basel), 1954, vol. XIV.
33. Barth, K. "Mein Verhältnis zu S. Kierkegaard", *Orbis Litterarum* (Kopenhagen), 1963, vol. XVIII, # 3–4.

34. Bense M. *Sören Kierkegaard: Leben im Geist*, Hamburg, 1942.
35. Blackham, H. J. *Six Existentialist Thinkers*, London, 1953.
36. Blanshard, B. "Kierkegaard on Faith", *The Personalist* (Los Angeles), 1968, vol. 49, # 1.
37. Blanshard, B. *Reason and Analysis*, London, 1956.
38. Bogen, I. "Remarks on the Kierkegaard–Hegel Controversy", *Synthese* (Dordrecht), 1961, vol. XIII, # 4.
39. Brun, I. "Feuerbach et Kierkegaard", *Cahiers du Sud* (Paris), 1963, # 371.
40. Brunner, E. *Offenbarung und Vernunft*, 1941.
41. Collins, J. *The Mind of Kierkegaard*, Chicago, 1953.
42. Diem, H. *Sören Kierkegaard: Spion im Dienste Gottes*, Frankfurt a. M., 1957.
43. Fischer, F. C. *Existenz und Innerlichkeit*, München, 1969.
44. Garelick, H. M. *The Antichristianity of Kierkegaard*, Den Haag, 1965.
45. Geismar, E. *Sören Kierkegaard*, Göttingen, 1929.
46. Gerdes, H. *Sören Kierkegaard: Leben und Werk*, Berlin, 1966.
47. Gill, I. H., ed. *Essays on Kierkegaard*, Minneapolis, 1969.
48. Gilson, E. *Recent Philosophy*, New York, 1966.
49. Glockner, H. "Hegelrenaissance und Neuhegelianismus", *Logos*, 1931, vol. XX, Heft 2.
50. Grimault, M. *La mélancolie de Kierkegaard*, Paris, 1965.
51. Gusdorf, G. *Kierkegaard*, Paris, 1963.
52. Hegel, G. W. F. *Vorlesungen über die Philosophie der Religion*, Vol. I, Berlin, 1932.
53. Heinemann, F. *Neue Wege der Philosophie*, Leipzig, 1929.
54. Heinemann, F. *Die Philosophie im 20. Jahrhundert*, Stuttgart, 1959.
55. Heiss, R. *Die grossen Dialektiker des 19. Jahrhunderts*, Köln, 1963.
56. Henriksen, A. *Method and Results of Kierkegaard Studies in Scandinavia*, Copenhagen, 1951.
57. Höffding, H. *S. Kierkegaard als Philosoph*, Stuttgart, 1902.
58. Hohlenberg, I. *Sören Kierkegaard*, London, 1954.
59. Holm, S. *Kierkegaards Geschichtsphilosophie*, Stuttgart, 1956.
60. Jaspers, K. *Aneignung und Polemik*, München, 1968.
61. Jaspers, K. *Philosophie*, Berlin, 1956.
62. Jaspers, K. "Schelling's Grösse und sein Verhängnis", *Studia philosophica* (Basel), 1954, vol. XIV.
63. Johansen, U. "Kierkegaard und Hegel", *Zeitschrift für philosophische Forschung* (Meisenheim), 1953, Heft 1.
64. Jolivet, R. *Introduction à Kierkegaard*, Paris, 1946.
65. Jolivet, R. *Kierkegaard: Aux sources de l'existentialisme chrétien*, Paris, 1958.
66. Kampits, P. "Leo Gabriel: Existenzphilosophie", *Philosophischer Literaturanzeiger* (Meisenheim), 1969, vol. 22, Heft 4.
67. *Kierkegaardiana*, Köbenhavn.
68. *Kierkegaard vivant*, Paris, 1966.
69. Kleine, G. "Marx and Kierkegaard"; in Lobkowicz, N., ed., *Marx and the Western World*, Notre Dame, 1967.
70. Koch, A. *Philosophy for the Time of Crisis*, New York, 1959.
71. Koktanek, A. M. *Schellings Seinslehre und Kierkegaard*, München, 1962.
72. Krieger, L. "History and Existentialism in Sartre", *The Critical Spirit*, Boston, 1967.
73. Lessing, A. "Hegel and Existentialism", *The Personalist* (Los Angeles), 1968, vol. 49, # 1.
74. Linke, P. F. *Niedererscheinungen in der Philosophie der Gegenwart*, München, 1961.
75. Litt, Th. *Hegel*, Heidelberg, 1953.
76. Löwith, K. *Von Hegel zu Nietzsche*, Stuttgart, 1964.
77. Lowrie, W. *Kierkegaard*, New York, 1962.
78. Lukács, G. *Die Zerstörung der Vernunft*, Berlin, 1954.
79. Mesnard, P. *Kierkegaard, sa vie, son oeuvre*, Paris, 1963.

80. Mora, J.-F. *Philosophy Today*, New York, 1960.
81. Nadler, K. "Hamann und Hegel", *Logos* (Tübingen), 1931, vol. XX, Heft 2.
82. Noack, H. *Die Philosophie Westeuropas im 20. Jahrhundert*, Basel, 1962.
83. Noack, L. *Philosophie-geschichtliches Lexikon*, Leipzig, 1879.
84. *Orbis Litterarum* (Köbenhavn), 1963, vol. XVIII, # 1–2.
85. Paulsen, A. *S. Kierkegaard: Deuter unserer Existenz*, Hamburg, 1955.
86. Price, G. *The Narrow Pass*, New York, 1963.
87. Prosch, H. *The Genesis of Twentieth Century Philosophy*, New York, 1966.
88. Rademacher, H. *Kierkegaard's Hegelverstandnis*, Köln, 1958.
89. Rohde, P. P. *S. Kierkegaard in Selbstdarstellungen und Bilddokumenten*, Reinbeck, 1959.
90. Rubiczek, P. *Existentialism, For and Against*, Cambridge, 1966.
91. Schrader, G. "Kant and Kierkegaard on Duty and Inclination", *Journal of Philosophy* (New York), 1968, # 21.
92. Schulz, W. "Die Vollendung des deutschen Idealismus in der Spätphilosophie Schelling's," *Studia philosophica* (Basel), 1954, vol. XIV.
93. Thompson, I. *The Lonely Labyrinth*, Illinois, 1967.
94. Thust, H. *S. Kierkegaard*, München, 1931.
95. Von Hagen, E. *Abstraktion und Konkretion bei Hegel und Kierkegaard*, Bonn, 1969.
96. Wahl, J. *Etudes Kierkegaardiennes*, Paris, 1949.
97. Wahl, J. *Les philosophies de l'existence*, Paris, 1954.
98. Wahl, J. "Espoir et désespoir chez Kierkegaard", *Cahiers du Sud* (Paris), 1963, # 371.
99. Wild, J. D. *The Challenge of Existentialism*, Bloomington, 1955.
100. Wilson, C. *Introduction to the New Existentialism*, London, 1966.

ABOUT THE AUTHOR

Bernard Emmanuilovich Bykhovskii (b. 1898) is a doctor of philosophical sciences and professor of the chair of philosophy at the Plekhanov Institute of National Economy, Moscow. He is well known as the author of one of the first textbooks on dialectical materialism (1930), and a number of monographs and pamphlets:

Enemies and Falsifiers of Marxism, Moscow, 1933.
The Philosophy of Descartes, Moscow, 1940.
The Method and System of Hegel, Moscow, 1941.
The Decay of Contemporary Bourgeois Philosophy, Moscow, 1947.
American Personalism, Moscow, 1948.
Basic Trends in Contemporary Idealist Philosophy, Moscow, 1957.
The Philosophy of Neo-Pragmatism, Moscow, 1959.
Personality and Society, Copenhagen, 1963.
Science, Society and the Future, Buenos Aires, 1965.
Ludwig Feuerbach, Moscow, 1967.
George Berkeley, Moscow, 1970.

B. E. Bykhovskii is a laureate of the USSR State Prize (1943) for his authorship and editing of vols. 1–3 of the *History of Philosophy*. This present book of his, *Kierkegaard*, was published in Moscow by Mysl in 1972.

PHILOSOPHICAL CURRENTS

BACKLIST

Vol. 1. Edward D'Angelo, *The Teaching of Critical Thinking*. Amsterdam, 1971.
Vol. 2. Hae Soo Pyun, *Nature, Intelligibility, and Metaphysics: Studies in the Philosophy of F.J.E. Woodbridge*. Amsterdam, 1972.
Vol. 3. Paul K. Crosser, *War Is Obsolete: The Dialectics of Military Technology and Its Consequences*. Amsterdam, 1972.
Vol. 4. Benjamin B. Page, *The Czechoslovak Reform Movement, 1963-1968. A Study in the Theory of Socialism*. Amsterdam, 1973.
Vol. 5. Paul K. Crosser/David H. DeGrood & Dale Riepe, *East-West Dialogues: Foundations and Problems of Revolutionary Praxis*. Amsterdam, 1973.
Vol. 6. Shingo Shibata, *Lessons of the Vietnam War: Philosophical Considerations on the Vietnam Revolution*. Amsterdam, 1973.
Vol. 7. Ralph M. Faris, *Revisionist Marxism: The Opposition Within*. Amsterdam, 1974.
Vol. 8. Howard L. Parsons, *Man East and West: Essays in East-West Philosophy*. Amsterdam, 1975.
Vol. 9. Max Rieser, *Messianism and Ephiphany: An Essay on the Origins of Christianity*. Amsterdam, 1973.
Vol. 10. William L. Rosensohn, *The Phenomenology of Charles S. Peirce: From the Doctrine of Categories to Phaneroscopy*. Amsterdam. 1974.
Vol. 11. Shingo Shibata. *Phoenix: Letters and Documents of Alice Herz*. Amsterdam, 1976.
Vol. 12. Philip M. Zeltner. *John Dewey's Aesthetic Philosophy*. Amsterdam, 1975.
Vol. 13. Fred J. Carrier. *The Third World Revolution*. Amsterdam, 1976.
Vol. 14. Henri Wald. *Introduction to Dialectical Logic*. Amsterdam, 1975.
Vol. 15. David H. DeGrood. *Consciousness and Social Life*. Amsterdam, 1976.

The series will be continued, standing orders for forthcoming volumes accepted.
Leaflet with full description free on request.
All volumes are available.

B. R. Grüner Publishing Co.
P. O. Box 70020
Nieuwe Herengracht 31
Amsterdam (Holland)